CONSCIOUS HUMAN ACTION

Is man free in action and thought, or is he bound by an iron necessity? There are few questions on which so much ingenuity has been expended. The idea of freedom has found enthusiastic supporters and stubborn opponents in plenty. There are those who, in their moral fervour, label anyone a man of limited intelligence who can deny so patent a fact as freedom. Opposed to them are others who regard it as the acme of unscientific thinking for anyone to believe that the uniformity of natural law is broken in the sphere of human action and thought. One and the same thing is thus proclaimed, now as the most precious possession of humanity, now as its most fatal illusion. Infinite subtlety has been employed to explain how human freedom can be consistent with determinism in nature of which man, after all, is a part. Others have been at no less pains to explain how such a delusion as this could have arisen. That we are dealing here with one of the most important questions for life, religion, conduct, science, must be clear to every one whose most prominent trait of character is not the reverse of thoroughness. It is one of the sad signs of the superficiality of present-day thought, that a book which attempts to develop a new faith out of the results of recent scientific research (David Friedrich Strauss, *Deralteund neueGlaube*), has nothing more to say on this question than these words: "With the question of the freedom of the human will we are not concerned. The alleged freedom of indifferent choice has been recognised as an empty illusion by every philosophy worthy of the name. The determination of the moral value of human conduct and character remains untouched by this problem." It is not because I consider that the book in which it occurs has any special importance that I quote this passage, but because it seems to me to express the only view to which the thought of the majority of our contemporaries is able to rise in this matter. Every one who has grown beyond the kindergarten-stage of science appears to know nowadays that freedom cannot consist in choosing, at one's pleasure, one or other of two possible courses of action. There is always, so we are told, a perfectly definite reason why, out of several possible actions, we carry out just one and no other.

This seems quite obvious. Nevertheless, down to the present day, the main attacks of the opponents of freedom are directed only against freedom of choice. Even Herbert Spencer, in fact, whose doctrines are gaining ground daily, says, "That every one is at liberty to desire or not to desire, which is the real proposition involved in the dogma of free will, is negatived as much by the analysis of consciousness, as by the contents of the preceding chapters" (*ThePrinciplesofPsychology*, Part IV, chap. ix, par. 219). Others, too, start from the same point of view in combating the concept of free will. The germs of all the relevant arguments are to be found as early as Spinoza. All that he brought forward in clear and simple language against the idea of freedom has since been repeated times without number, but as a rule enveloped in the most sophisticated arguments, so that it is difficult to recognise the straightforward train of thought which is alone in question. Spinoza writes in a letter of October or November, 1674, "I call a thing free which exists and acts from the pure necessity of its nature, and I call that unfree, of which the being and action are precisely and fixedly determined by something else. Thus, *e.g.*, God, though necessary, is free because he exists only through the necessity of his own nature. Similarly, God knows himself and all else as free, because it follows solely from the necessity of his nature that he knows all. You see, therefore, that for me freedom consists not in free decision, but in free necessity.

"But let us come down to created things which are all determined by external causes to exist and to act in a fixed and definite manner. To perceive this more clearly, let us imagine a perfectly simple case. A stone, for example, receives from an external cause acting upon it a certain quantity of motion, by reason of which it necessarily continues to move, after the impact of the external cause has ceased. The continued motion of the stone is due to compulsion, not to the necessity of its own nature, because it requires to be defined by the impact of an external cause. What is true here for the stone is true also for every other particular thing, however complicated and many-sided it may be, namely, that everything is necessarily determined by external causes to exist and to act in a fixed and definite manner.

"Now, pray, assume that this stone during its motion thinks and knows that it is striving to the best of its power to continue in motion. This stone which is conscious only of its striving and is by no means indifferent, will believe that it is absolutely free, and that it continues in motion for no other reason than its own will to continue. Now this is that human freedom which everybody claims to possess and which consists in nothing but this, that men are conscious of their desires, but ignorant of the causes by which they are determined. Thus the child believes that he desires milk of his own free will, the angry boy regards his desire for vengeance as free, and the coward his desire for flight. Again, the drunken man believes that he says of his own free will what, sober again, he would fain have left unsaid, and as this prejudice is innate in all men, it is difficult to free oneself from it. For, although experience teaches us often enough that man least of all can temper his desires, and that, moved by conflicting passions, he perceives the better and pursues the worse, yet he considers himself free because there are some things which he desires less strongly, and some desires which he can easily inhibit through the recollection of something else which it is often possible to recall."

It is easy to detect the fundamental error of this view, because it is so clearly and definitely expressed. The same necessity by which a stone makes a definite movement as the result of an impact, is said to compel a man to carry out an action when impelled thereto by any cause. It is only because man is conscious of his action, that he thinks himself to be its originator. In doing so, he overlooks the fact that he is driven by a cause which he must obey unconditionally. The error in this train of thought is easily brought to light. Spinoza, and all who think like him, overlook the fact that man not only is conscious of his action, but also may become conscious of the cause which guides him. Anyone can see that a child is not free when he desires milk, nor the drunken man when he says things which he later regrets. Neither knows anything of the causes, working deep within their organisms, which exercise irresistible control over them. But is it justifiable to lump together actions of this kind with those in which a man is conscious not only of his actions but also of their causes? Are the actions of men really all of one kind? Should the act of a soldier on the field of battle, of the scientific researcher in his laboratory, of the statesman in the most complicated diplomatic negotiations, be placed on the same level with that of the child when he desires milk? It is, no doubt, true that it is best to seek the solution of a problem where the conditions are simplest. But lack of ability to see distinctions has before now caused endless confusion. There is, after all, a profound difference between knowing the motive of my action and not knowing it. At first sight this seems a self-evident truth. And yet the opponents of freedom never ask themselves whether a motive of action which I recognise and understand, is to be regarded as compulsory for me in the same sense as the organic process which causes the child to cry for milk.

Eduard von Hartmann, in his *PhänomenologiedesSittlichenBewusstseins* (p. 451), asserts that the human will depends on two chief factors, the motives and the character. If one regards men as all alike, or at any rate the differences between them as negligible, then their will appears as determined from without, viz., by the circumstances with which they come in contact. But if one bears in mind that men adopt an idea as the motive of their conduct, only if their character is such that this idea arouses a desire in them, then men appear as determined from within and not from without. Now, because an idea, given to us from without, must first in accordance with our characters be adopted as a motive, men believe that they are free, i.e., independent of external influences. The truth, however, according to Eduard von Hartmann, is that "even though we must first adopt an idea as a motive, we do so not arbitrarily, but according to the disposition of our characters, that is, we are anything but free." Here again the difference between motives, which I allow to influence me only after I have consciously made them my own, and those which I follow without any clear knowledge of them, is absolutely ignored.

This leads us straight to the standpoint from which the subject will be treated here. Have we any right to consider the question of the freedom of the will by itself at all? And if not, with what other question must it necessarily be connected?

If there is a difference between conscious and unconscious motives of action, then the action in which the former issue should be judged differently from the action which springs from blind impulse. Hence our first question will concern this difference, and on the result of this inquiry will depend what attitude we ought to take up towards the question of freedom proper.

What does it mean to have knowledge of the motives of one's actions? Too little attention has been paid to this question, because, unfortunately, man who is an indivisible whole has always been torn asunder by us. The agent has been divorced from the knower, whilst he who matters more than everything else, viz., the man who acts because he knows, has been utterly overlooked.

It is said that man is free when he is controlled only by his reason, and not by his animal passions. Or, again, that to be free means to be able to determine one's life and action by purposes and deliberate decisions.

Nothing is gained by assertions of this sort. For the question is just whether reason, purposes, and decisions exercise the same kind of compulsion over a man as his animal passions. If, without my doing, a rational decision occurs in me with the same necessity with which hunger and thirst happen to me, then I must needs obey it, and my freedom is an illusion.

Another form of expression runs: to be free means, not that we can will what we will, but that we can do what we will. This thought has been expressed with great clearness by the poet-philosopher Robert Hamerling in his *AtomistikdesW illens*. "Man can, it is true, do what he wills, but he cannot will what he wills, because his will is determined by motives! He cannot will what he wills? Let us consider these phrases more closely. Have they any intelligible meaning? Does freedom of will, then, mean being able to will without ground, without motive? What does willing mean if not to have grounds for doing, or striving to do, this rather than that? To will anything without ground or motive would mean to will something without willing it. The concept of motive is indissolubly bound up with that of will. Without the determining motive the will is an empty faculty; it is the motive which makes it active and real. It is, therefore, quite true that the human will is not 'free,' inasmuch as its direction is always determined by the strongest motive. But, on the other hand, it must be admitted that it is absurd to speak, in contrast with this 'unfreedom,' of a conceivable 'freedom' of the will, which would consist in being able to will what one does not will" (*AtomistikdesW illens*, p. 213 ff.).

Here, again, only motives in general are mentioned, without taking into account the difference between unconscious and conscious motives. If a motive affects me, and I am compelled to act on it because it proves to be the "strongest" of its kind, then the idea of freedom ceases to have any meaning. How should it matter to me whether I can do a thing or not, if I am forced by the motive to do it? The primary question is, not whether I can do a thing or not when impelled by a motive, but whether the only motives are such as impel me with absolute necessity. If I must will something, then I may well be absolutely indifferent as to whether I can also do it. And if, through my character, or through circumstances prevailing in my environment, a motive is forced on me which to my thinking is unreasonable, then I should even have to be glad if I could not do what I will.

The question is, not whether I can carry out a decision once made, but how I come to make the decision.

What distinguishes man from all other organic beings is his rational thought. Activity is common to him with other organisms. Nothing is gained by seeking analogies in the animal world to clear up the concept of freedom as applied to the actions of human beings. Modern science loves these analogies. When scientists have succeeded in finding among animals something similar to human behaviour, they believe they have touched on the most important question of the science of man. To what misunderstandings this view leads is seen, for example, in the book *Die IllusionderW illensfreiheit*, by P. Ree, 1885, where, on Page 5, the following remark on freedom appears: "It is easy to explain why the movement of a stone seems to us necessary, while the volition of a donkey does not. The causes which set the stone in motion are external and visible, while the causes which determine the donkey's volition are internal and invisible. Between us and the place of their activity there is the skull cap of the ass…. The causal nexus is not visible and is therefore thought to be non-existent. The volition, it is explained, is, indeed, the cause of the donkey's turning round, but is itself unconditioned; it is an absolute beginning." Here again human actions in which there is a consciousness of the motives are simply ignored, for Ree declares, "that between us and the sphere of their activity there is the skull cap of the ass." As these words show, it has not so much as dawned on Ree that there are actions, not indeed of the ass, but of human beings, in which the motive, become conscious, lies between us and the action. Ree demonstrates his blindness once again a few pages further on, when he says, "We do not perceive the causes by which our will is determined, hence we think it is not causally determined at all."

But enough of examples which prove that many argue against freedom without knowing in the least what freedom is.

That an action of which the agent does not know why he performs it, cannot be free goes without saying. But what of the freedom of an action about the motives of which we reflect? This leads us to the question of the origin and meaning of thought. For without the recognition of the activity of mind which is called thought, it is impossible to understand what is meant either by knowledge of something or by action. When we know what thought in general means, it will be easier to see clearly the role which thought plays in human action. As Hegel rightly says, "It is thought which turns the soul, common to us and animals, into spirit." Hence it is thought which we may expect to give to human action its characteristic stamp.

I do not mean to imply that all our actions spring only from the sober deliberations of our reason. I am very far from calling only those actions "human" in the highest sense, which proceed from abstract judgments. But as soon as our conduct rises above the sphere of the satisfaction of purely animal desires, our motives are always shaped by thoughts. Love, pity, and patriotism are motives of action which cannot be analysed away into cold concepts of the understanding. It is said that here the heart, the soul, hold sway. This is no doubt true. But the heart and the soul create no motives. They presuppose them. Pity enters my heart when the thought of a person who arouses pity had appeared in my consciousness. The way to the heart is through the head. Love is no exception. Whenever it is not merely the expression of bare sexual instinct, it depends on the thoughts we form of the loved one. And the more we idealise the loved one in our thoughts, the more blessed is our love. Here, too, thought is the father of feeling. It is said that love makes us blind to the failings of the loved one. But the opposite view can be taken, namely that it is precisely for the good points that love opens the eyes. Many pass by these good points without notice. One, however, perceives them, and just because he does, love awakens in his soul. What else has he done except perceive what hundreds have failed to see? Love is not theirs, because they lack the perception.

From whatever point we regard the subject, it becomes more and more clear that the question of the nature of human action presupposes that of the origin of thought. I shall, therefore, turn next to this question.

II

WHY THE DESIRE FOR KNOWLEDGE IS FUNDAMENTAL

> Zwei Seelen wohnen, ach! in meiner Brust,
> Die eine will sich von der andern trennen;
> Die eine hält, in derber Liebeslust,
> Sich an die Welt mit klammernden Organen;
> Die andre hebt gewaltsam sich vom Dust
> Zu den Gefilden hoher Ahnen.[1]
>
> Faust I, 1112–1117.

In these words Goethe expresses a trait which is deeply ingrained in human nature. Man is not a self-contained unity. He demands ever more than the world, of itself, offers him. Nature has endowed us with needs; among them are some the satisfaction of which she leaves to our own activity. However abundant the gifts which we have received, still more abundant are our desires. We seem born to dissatisfaction. And our desire for knowledge is but a special instance of this unsatisfied striving. Suppose we look twice at a tree. The first time we see its branches at rest, the second time in motion. We are not satisfied with this observation. Why, we ask, does the tree appear to us now at rest, then in motion? Every glance at nature evokes in us a multitude of questions. Every phenomenon we meet presents a new problem to be solved. Every experience is to us a riddle. We observe that from the egg there emerges a creature like the mother animal, and we ask for the reason of the likeness. We observe a living being grow and develop to a determinate degree of perfection, and we seek the conditions of this experience. Nowhere are we satisfied with the facts which nature spreads out before our senses. Everywhere we seek what we call the explanation of these facts.

The something more which we seek in things, over and above what is immediately given to us in them, splits our whole being into two parts. We become conscious of our opposition to the world. We oppose ourselves to the world as independent beings. The universe has for us two opposite poles: Self and World.

We erect this barrier between ourselves and the world as soon as consciousness is first kindled in us. But we never cease to feel that, in spite of all, we belong to the world, that there is a connecting link between it and us, and that we are beings within, and not without, the universe.

This feeling makes us strive to bridge over this opposition, and ultimately the whole spiritual striving of mankind is nothing but the bridging of this opposition. The history of our spiritual life is a continuous seeking after union between ourselves and the world. Religion, Art, and Science follow, one and all, this goal. The religious man seeks in the revelation, which God grants him, the solution of the world problem, which his Self, dissatisfied with the world of mere phenomena, sets him as a task. The artist seeks to embody in his material the ideas which are his Self, that he may thus reconcile the spirit which lives within him and the outer world. He, too, feels dissatisfied with the world of mere appearances, and seeks to mould into it that something more which his Self supplies and which transcends appearances. The thinker searches for the laws of phenomena. He strives to master by thought what he experiences by observation. Only when we have transformed the world-content into our thought-content do we recapture the connection which we had ourselves broken off. We shall see later that this goal can be reached only if we penetrate much more deeply than is often done into the nature of the scientist's problem. The whole situation, as I have here stated it, meets us, on the stage of history, in the conflict between the one-world theory, or Monism, and the two-world theory, or Dualism. Dualism pays attention only to the separation between the Self and the World, which the consciousness of man has brought about. All its efforts consist in a vain struggle to reconcile these opposites, which it calls now Mind and Matter, now Subject and Object, now Thought and Appearance. The Dualist feels that there must be a bridge between the two worlds, but is not able to find it. In so far as man is aware of himself as "I," he cannot but put down this "I" in thought on the side of Spirit; and in opposing to this "I" the world, he is bound to reckon on the world's side the realm of percepts given to the senses, i.e., the Material World. In doing so, man assigns a position to himself within this very antithesis of Spirit and Matter. He is the more compelled to do so because his own body belongs to the Material World. Thus the "I," or Ego, belongs as a part to the realm of Spirit; the material objects and processes which are perceived by the senses belong to the "World." All the riddles which belong to Spirit and Matter, man must inevitably rediscover in the fundamental riddle of his own nature. Monism pays attention only to the unity and tries either to deny or to slur over the opposites, present though they are. Neither of these two points of view can satisfy us, for they do not do justice to the facts. The Dualist sees in Mind (Self) and Matter (World) two essentially different entities, and cannot therefore understand how they can interact with one another. How should Mind be aware of what goes on in Matter, seeing that the essential nature of Matter is quite alien to Mind? Or how in these circumstances should Mind act upon Matter, so as to translate its intentions into actions? The most absurd hypotheses have been propounded to answer these questions. However, up to the present the Monists are not in a much better position. They have tried three different ways of meeting the difficulty. Either they deny Mind and become Materialists; or they deny Matter in order to seek their salvation as Spiritualists; or they assert that, even in the simplest entities in the world, Mind and Matter are indissolubly bound together, so that there is no need to marvel at the appearance in man of these two modes of existence, seeing that they are never found apart.

Materialism can never offer a satisfactory explanation of the world. For every attempt at an explanation must begin with the formation of thoughts about the phenomena of the world. Materialism, thus, begins with the thought of Matter or material processes. But, in doing so, it is *ipso facto* confronted by two different sets of facts, viz., the material world and the thoughts about it. The Materialist seeks to make these latter intelligible by regarding them as purely material processes. He believes that thinking takes place in the brain, much in the same way that digestion takes place in the animal organs. Just as he ascribes mechanical, chemical, and organic processes to Nature, so he credits her in certain circumstances with the capacity to think. He overlooks that, in doing so, he is merely shifting the problem from one place to another. Instead of to himself he ascribes the power of thought to Matter. And thus he is back again at his starting-point.

How does Matter come to think of its own nature? Why is it not simply satisfied with itself and content to accept its own existence? The Materialist has turned his attention away from the definite subject, his own self, and occupies himself with an indefinite shadowy somewhat. And here the old problem meets him again. The materialistic theory cannot solve the problem; it can only shift it to another place.

What of the Spiritualistic theory? The pure Spiritualist denies to Matter all independent existence and regards it merely as a product of Spirit. But when he tries to apply this theory to the solution of the riddle of his own human nature, he finds himself caught in a tight place. Over against the "I," or Ego, which can be ranged on the side of Spirit, there stands directly the world of the senses. No spiritual approach to it seems open. It has to be perceived and experienced by the Ego with the help of material processes. Such material processes the Ego does not discover in itself, so long as it regards its own nature as exclusively spiritual. From all that it achieves by its own spiritual effort, the sensible world is ever excluded. It seems as if the Ego had to concede that the world would be a closed book to it, unless it could establish a non-spiritual relation to the world. Similarly, when it comes to acting, we have to translate our purposes into realities with the help of material things and forces. We are, therefore, dependent on the outer world. The most extreme Spiritualist, or, if you prefer it, Idealist, is Johann Gottlieb Fichte. He attempts to deduce the whole edifice of the world from the "Ego." What he has actually accomplished is a magnificent thought-picture of the world, without any empirical content. As little as it is possible for the Materialist to argue the Mind away, just as little is it possible for the Idealist to do without the outer world of Matter.

When man directs his theoretical reflection upon the Ego, he perceives, in the first instance, only the work of the Ego in the conceptual elaboration of the world of ideas. Hence a philosophy the direction of which is spiritualistic, may feel tempted, in view of man's own essential nature, to acknowledge nothing of spirit except this world of ideas. In this way Spiritualism becomes one-sided Idealism. Instead of going on to penetrate through the world of ideas to the spiritual world, idealism identifies the spiritual world with the world of ideas itself. As a result, it is compelled to remain fixed with its world-view in the circle of the activity of the Ego, as if it were bewitched.

A curious variant of Idealism is to be found in the theory which F. A. Lange has put forward in his widely read *History of Materialism*. He holds that the Materialists are quite right in declaring all phenomena, including our thoughts, to be the product of purely material processes, but, in turn, Matter and its processes are for him themselves the product of our thinking. "The senses give us only the effects of things, not true copies, much less the things themselves. But among these mere effects we must include the senses themselves together with the brain and the molecular vibrations which we assume to go on there." That is, our thinking is produced by the material processes, and these by our thinking. Lange's philosophy is thus nothing more than the philosophical analogon of the story of honest Baron Münchhausen, who holds himself up in the air by his own pigtail.

The third form of Monism is that which finds even in the simplest real (the atom) the union of both Matter and Mind. But nothing is gained by this either, except that the question, the origin of which is really in our consciousness, is shifted to another place. How comes it that the simple real manifests itself in a two-fold manner, if it is an indivisible unity?

Against all these theories we must urge the fact that we meet with the basal and fundamental opposition first in our own consciousness. It is we ourselves who break away from the bosom of Nature and contrast ourselves as Self with the World. Goethe has given classic expression to this in his essay *Nature*. "Living in the midst of her (Nature) we are strangers to her. Ceaselessly she speaks to us, yet betrays none of her secrets." But Goethe knows the reverse side too: "Mankind is all in her, and she in all mankind."

However true it may be that we have estranged ourselves from Nature, it is none the less true that we feel we are in her and belong to her. It can be only her own life which pulses also in us.

We must find the way back to her again. A simple reflection may point this way out to us. We have, it is true, torn ourselves away from Nature, but we must none the less have carried away something of her in our own selves. This quality of Nature in us we must seek out, and then we shall discover our connection with her once more. Dualism neglects to do this. It considers the human mind as a spiritual entity utterly alien to Nature and attempts somehow to hitch it on to Nature. No wonder that it cannot find the coupling link. We can find Nature outside of us only if we have first learnt to know her within us. The Natural within us must be our guide to her. This marks out our path of inquiry. We shall attempt no speculations concerning the interaction of Mind and Matter. We shall rather probe into the depths of our own being, to find there those elements which we saved in our flight from Nature.

The examination of our own being must bring the solution of the problem. We must reach a point where we can say, "This is no longer merely 'I,' this is something which is more than 'I.'"

I am well aware that many who have read thus far will not consider my discussion in keeping with "the present state of science." To such criticism I can reply only that I have so far not been concerned with any scientific results, but simply with the description of what every one of us experiences in his own consciousness. That a few phrases have slipped in about attempts to reconcile Mind and the World has been due solely to the desire to elucidate the actual facts. I have therefore made no attempt to give to the expressions "Self," "Mind," "World," "Nature," the precise meaning which they usually bear in Psychology and Philosophy. The ordinary consciousness ignores the sharp distinctions of the sciences, and so far my purpose has been solely to record the facts of everyday experience. I am concerned, not with the way in which science, so far, has interpreted consciousness, but with the way in which we experience it in every moment of our lives.

1

> Two souls, alas! reside within my breast,
> And each withdraws from, and repels, its brother.
> One with tenacious organs holds in love

And clinging lust the world in its embraces;
The other strongly sweeps, this dust above,
Into the high ancestral spaces.

Faust, Part I, Scene 2.

(Bayard Taylor's translation.)

III

THOUGHT AS THE INSTRUMENT OF KNOWLEDGE

When I observe how a billiard ball, when struck, communicates its motion to another, I remain entirely without influence on the process before me. The direction and velocity of the motion of the second ball is determined by the direction and velocity of the first. As long as I remain a mere spectator, I can say nothing about the motion of the second ball until after it has happened. It is quite different when I begin to reflect on the content of my observations. The purpose of my reflection is to construct concepts of the process. I connect the concept of an elastic ball with certain other concepts of mechanics, and consider the special circumstances which obtain in the instance in question. I try, in other words, to add to the process which takes place without my interference, a second process which takes place in the conceptual sphere. This latter process is dependent on me. This is shown by the fact that I can rest content with the observation, and renounce all search for concepts if I have no need of them. If, therefore, this need is present, then I am not content until I have established a definite connection among the concepts, ball, elasticity, motion, impact, velocity, etc., so that they apply to the observed process in a definite way. As surely as the occurrence of the observed process is independent of me, so surely is the occurrence of the conceptual process dependent on me.

We shall have to consider later whether this activity of mine really proceeds from my own independent being, or whether those modern physiologists are right who say that we cannot think as we will, but that we must think exactly as the thoughts and thought-connections determine, which happen to be in our minds at any given moment. (*Cp.* Ziehen, *Leitfaden der Physiologischen Psychologie,* Jena, 1893, p. 171.) For the present we wish merely to establish the fact that we constantly feel obliged to seek for concepts and connections of concepts, which stand in definite relation to the objects and processes which are given independently of us. Whether this activity is really ours, or whether we are determined to it by an unalterable necessity, is a question which we need not decide at present. What is unquestionable is that the activity appears, in the first instance, to be ours. We know for certain that concepts are not given together with the objects to which they correspond. My being the agent in the conceptual process may be an illusion; but there is no doubt that to immediate observation I appear to be active. Our present question is, what do we gain by supplementing a process with a conceptual counterpart?

There is a far-reaching difference between the ways in which, for me, the parts of a process are related to one another before, and after, the discovery of the corresponding concepts. Mere observation can trace the parts of a given process as they occur, but their connection remains obscure without the help of concepts. I observe the first billiard ball move towards the second in a certain direction and with a certain velocity. What will happen after the impact I cannot tell in advance. I can once more only watch it happen with my eyes. Suppose someone obstructs my view of the field where the process is happening, at the moment when the impact occurs, then, as mere spectator, I remain ignorant of what goes on. The situation is very different, if prior to the obstructing of my view I have discovered the concepts corresponding to the nexus of events. In that case I can say what occurs, even when I am no longer able to observe. There is nothing in a merely observed process or object to show its relation to other processes or objects. This relation becomes manifest only when observation is combined with thought.

Observation and thought are the two points of departure for all the spiritual striving of man, in so far as he is conscious of such striving. The workings of common sense, as well as the most complicated scientific researches, rest on these two fundamental pillars of our minds. Philosophers have started from various ultimate antitheses, Idea and Reality, Subject and Object, Appearance and Thing-in-itself, Ego and Non-Ego, Idea and Will, Concept and Matter, Force and Substance, the Conscious and the Unconscious. It is, however, easy to show that all these antitheses are subsequent to that between Observation and Thought, this being for man the most important.

Whatever principle we choose to lay down, we must either prove that somewhere we have observed it, or we must enunciate it in the form of a clear concept which can be re-thought by any other thinker. Every philosopher who sets out to discuss his fundamental principles, must express them in conceptual form and thus use thought. He therefore indirectly admits that his activity presupposes thought. We leave open here the question whether thought or something else is the chief factor in the development of the world. But it is at any rate clear that the philosopher can gain no knowledge of this development without thought. In the occurrence of phenomena thought may play a secondary part, but it is quite certain that it plays a chief part in the construction of a theory about them.

As regards observation, our need of it is due to our organisation. Our thought about a horse and the object "horse" are two things which for us have separate existences. The object is accessible to us only by means of observation. As little as we can construct a concept of a horse by mere staring at the animal, just as little are we able by mere thought to produce the corresponding object.

In time observation actually precedes thought. For we become familiar with thought itself in the first instance by observation. It was essentially a description of an observation when, at the beginning of this chapter, we gave an account of how thought is kindled by an objective process and transcends the merely given. Whatever enters the circle of our experiences becomes an object of apprehension to us first through observation. All contents of sensations, all perceptions, intuitions, feelings, acts of will, dreams and fancies, images, concepts, ideas, all illusions and hallucinations, are given to us through observation.

But thought as an object of observation differs essentially from all other objects. The observation of a table, or a tree, occurs in me as soon as those objects appear within the horizon of my field of consciousness. Yet I do not, at the same time, observe my thought about these things. I observe the table, but I carry on a process of thought about the table without at the same moment observing this thought-process. I must first take up a standpoint outside of my own activity, if I want to observe my thought about the table, as well as the table. Whereas the observation of things and processes, and the thinking about them, are everyday occurrences making up the continuous current of my life, the observation of the thought-process itself is an exceptional attitude to adopt. This fact must be taken into account, when we come to determine the relations of thought as an object of observation to all other objects. We must be quite clear about the fact that, in observing the thought-processes, we are applying to them a method which is our normal attitude in the study of all other objects in the world, but which in the ordinary course of that study is usually not applied to thought itself.

Someone might object that what I have said about thinking applies equally to feeling and to all other mental activities. Thus it is said that when, *e.g.*, I have a feeling of pleasure, the feeling is kindled by the object, but it is this object I observe, not the feeling of pleasure. This objection, however, is based on an error. Pleasure does not stand at all in the same relation to its object as the concept constructed by thought. I am conscious, in the most positive way, that the concept of a thing is formed through my activity; whereas a feeling of pleasure is produced in me by an object in a way similar to that in which, *e.g.*, a change is caused in an object by a stone which falls on it. For observation, a pleasure is given in exactly the same way as the event which causes it. The same is not true of concepts. I can ask why an event arouses in me a feeling of pleasure. But I certainly cannot ask why an occurrence causes in me a certain number of concepts. The question would be simply meaningless. In thinking about an occurrence, I am not concerned with it as an effect on me. I learn nothing about myself from knowing the concepts which correspond to the observed change caused in a pane of glass by a stone thrown against it. But I do learn something about myself when I know the feeling which a certain occurrence arouses in me. When I say of an object which I perceive, "this is a rose," I say absolutely nothing about myself; but when I say of the same thing that "it causes a feeling of pleasure in me," I characterise not only the rose, but also myself in my relation to the rose.

There can, therefore, be no question of putting thought and feeling on a level as objects of observation. And the same could easily be shown of other activities of the human mind. Unlike thought, they must be classed with any other observed objects or events. The peculiar nature of thought lies just in this, that it is an activity which is directed solely on the observed object and not on the thinking subject. This is apparent even from the way in which we express our thoughts about an object, as distinct from our feelings or acts of will. When I see an object and recognise it as a table, I do not as a rule say, "I am thinking of a table," but, "this is a table." On the other hand, I do say, "I am pleased with the table." In the former case, I am not at all interested in stating that I have entered into a relation with the table; whereas, in the second case, it is just this relation which matters. In saying, "I am thinking of a table," I adopt the exceptional point of view characterised above, in which something is made the object of observation which is always present in our mental activity, without being itself normally an observed object.

The peculiar nature of thought consists just in this, that the thinker forgets his thinking while actually engaged in it. It is not thinking which occupies his attention, but rather the object of thought which he observes.

The first point, then, to notice about thought is that it is the unobserved element in our ordinary mental life.

The reason why we do not notice the thinking which goes on in our ordinary mental life is no other than this, that it is our own activity. Whatever I do not myself produce appears in my field of consciousness as an object; I contrast it with myself as something the existence of which is independent of me. It forces itself upon me. I must accept it as the presupposition of my thinking. As long as I think about the object, I am absorbed in it, my attention is turned on it. To be thus absorbed in the object is just to contemplate it by thought. I attend, not to my activity, but to its object. In other words, whilst I am thinking I pay no heed to my thinking which is of my own making, but only to the object of my thinking which is not of my making.

I am, moreover, in exactly the same position when I adopt the exceptional point of view and think of my own thought-processes. I can never observe my present thought, I can only make my past experiences of thought-processes subsequently the objects of fresh thoughts. If I wanted to watch my present thought, I should have to split myself into two persons, one to think, the other to observe this thinking. But this is impossible. I can only accomplish it in two separate acts. The observed thought-processes are never those in which I am actually engaged but others. Whether, for this purpose, I make observations on my own former thoughts, or follow the thought-processes of another person, or finally, as in the example of the motions of the billiard balls, assume an imaginary thought-process, is immaterial.

There are two things which are incompatible with one another: productive activity and the theoretical contemplation of that activity. This is recognised even in the First Book of Moses. It represents God as creating the world in the first six days, and only after its completion is any contemplation of the world possible: "And God saw everything that he had made and, behold, it was very good." The same applies to our thinking. It must be there first, if we would observe it.

The reason why it is impossible to observe the thought-process in its actual occurrence at any given moment, is the same as that which makes it possible for us to know it more immediately and more intimately than any other process in the world. Just because it is our own creation do we know the characteristic features of its course, the manner in which the process, in detail, takes place. What in the other spheres of observation we can discover only indirectly, viz., the relevant objective nexus and the relations of the individual objects, that is known to us immediately in the case of thought. I do not know off-hand why, for perception, thunder follows lightning, but I know immediately, from the content of the two concepts, why my thought connects the concept of thunder with that of lightning. It does not matter for my argument whether my concepts of thunder and lightning are correct. The connection between the concepts I have is clear to me, and that through the very concepts themselves.

This transparent clearness in the observation of our thought-processes is quite independent of our knowledge of the physiological basis of thought. I am speaking here of thought in the sense in which it is the object of our observation of our own mental activity. For this purpose it is quite irrelevant how one material process in my brain causes or influences another, whilst I am carrying on a process of thought. What I observe, in studying a thought-process, is, not what process in my brain connects the concept of thunder with that of lightning, but what is my reason for bringing these two concepts into a definite relation. Introspection shows that, in linking thought with thought, I am guided by their content, not by the material processes in the brain. This remark would be quite superfluous in a less materialistic age than ours. To-day, however, when there are people who believe that, when we know what matter is, we shall know also how it thinks, it is necessary to affirm the possibility of speaking of thought without trespassing on the domain of brain physiology. Many people to-day find it difficult to grasp the concept of thought in its purity. Anyone who challenges the account of thought which I have given here, by quoting Cabanis' statement that "the brain secretes thoughts as the liver does gall or the spittle-glands spittle, etc." simply does not know of what I am talking. He attempts to discover thought by the same method of mere observation which we apply to the other objects that make up the world. But he cannot find it in this way, because, as I have shown, it eludes just this ordinary observation. Whoever cannot transcend Materialism lacks the ability to throw himself into the exceptional attitude I have described, in which he becomes conscious of what in all other mental activity remains unconscious. It is as useless to discuss thought with one who is not willing to adopt this attitude, as it would be to discuss colour with a blind man. Let him not imagine, however, that we regard physiological processes as thought. He fails to explain thought, because he is not even aware that it is there.

For every one, however, who has the ability to observe thought, and with good will every normal man has this ability, this observation is the most important he can make. For he observes something which he himself produces. He is not confronted by what is to begin with a strange object, but by his own activity. He knows how that which he observes has come to be. He perceives clearly its connections and relations. He gains a firm point from which he can, with well-founded hopes, seek an explanation of the other phenomena of the world.

The feeling that he had found such a firm foundation, induced the father of modern philosophy, Descartes, to base the whole of human knowledge on the principle, "I think, therefore I am." All other things, all other processes, are independent of me. Whether they be truth, or illusion, or dream, I know not. There is only one thing of which I am absolutely certain, for I myself am the author of its indubitable existence; and that is my thought. Whatever other origin it may have in addition, whether it come from God or from elsewhere, of one thing I am sure, that it exists in the sense that I myself produce it. Descartes had, to begin with, no justification for reading any other meaning into his principle. All he had a right to assert was that, in apprehending myself as thinking, I apprehend myself, within the world-system, in that activity which is most uniquely characteristic of me. What the added words "therefore I am" are intended to mean has been much debated. They can have a meaning on one condition only. The simplest assertion I can make of a thing is, that it is, that it exists. What kind of existence, in detail, it has, can in no case be determined on the spot, as soon as the thing enters within the horizon of my experience. Each object must be studied in its relations to others, before we can determine the sense in which we can speak of its existence. An experienced process may be a complex of percepts, or it may be a dream, an hallucination, etc. In short, I cannot say in what sense it exists. I can never read off the kind of existence from the process itself, for I can discover it only when I consider the process in its relation to other things. But this, again, yields me no knowledge beyond just its relation to other things. My inquiry touches firm ground only when I find an object, the reason of the existence of which I can gather from itself. Such an object I am myself in so far as I think, for I qualify my existence by the determinate and self-contained content of my thought-activity. From here I can go on to ask whether other things exist in the same or in some other sense.

When thought is made an object of observation, something which usually escapes our attention is added to the other observed contents of the world. But the usual manner of observation, such as is employed also for other objects, is in no way altered. We add to the number of objects of observation, but not to the number of methods. When we are observing other things, there enters among the world-processes—among which I now include observation—one process which is overlooked. There is present something different from every other kind of process, something which is not taken into account. But when I make an object of my own thinking, there is no such neglected element present. For what lurks now in the background is just thought itself over again. The object of observation is qualitatively identical with the activity directed upon it. This is another characteristic feature of thought-processes. When we make them objects of observation, we are not compelled to do so with the help of something qualitatively different, but can remain within the realm of thought.

When I weave a tissue of thoughts round an independently given object, I transcend my observation, and the question then arises, What right have I to do this? Why do I not passively let the object impress itself on me? How is it possible for my thought to be relevantly related to the object? These are questions which every one must put to himself who reflects on his own thought-processes. But all these questions lapse when we think about thought itself. We then add nothing to our thought that is foreign to it, and therefore have no need to justify any such addition.

Schelling says: "To know Nature means to create Nature." If we take these words of the daring philosopher of Nature literally, we shall have to renounce for ever all hope of gaining knowledge of Nature. For Nature after all exists, and if we have to create it over again, we must know the principles according to which it has originated in the first instance. We should have to borrow from Nature as it exists the conditions of existence for the Nature which we are about to create. But this borrowing, which would have to precede the creating, would be a knowing of Nature, and would be this even if after the borrowing no creation at all were attempted. The only kind of Nature which it would be possible to create without previous knowledge, would be a Nature different from the existing one.

What is impossible with Nature, viz., creation prior to knowledge, that we accomplish in the act of thought. Were we to refrain from thinking until we had first gained knowledge of it, we should never think at all. We must resolutely think straight ahead, and then afterwards by introspective analysis gain knowledge of our own processes. Thus we ourselves create the thought-processes which we then make objects of observation. The existence of all other objects is provided for us without any activity on our part.

My contention that we must think before we can make thought an object of knowledge, might easily be countered by the apparently equally valid contention that we cannot wait with digesting until we have first observed the process of digestion. This objection would be similar to that brought by Pascal against Descartes, when he asserted we might also say "I walk, therefore I am." Certainly I must digest resolutely and not wait until I have studied the physiological process of digestion. But I could only compare this with the analysis of thought if, after digestion, I set myself not to analyse it by thought, but to eat and digest it. It is not without reason that, while digestion cannot become the object of digestion, thought can very well become the object of thought.

This then is indisputable, that in thinking we have got hold of one bit of the world-process which requires our presence if anything is to happen. And that is the very point that matters. The very reason why things seem so puzzling is just that I play no part in their production. They are simply given to me, whereas I know how thought is produced. Hence there can be no more fundamental starting-point than thought from which to regard all world-processes.

I should like still to mention a widely current error which prevails with regard to thought. It is often said that thought, in its real nature, is never experienced. The thought-processes which connect our perceptions with one another, and weave about them a network of concepts, are not at all the same as those which our analysis afterwards extracts from the objects of perception, in order to make them the object of study. What we have unconsciously woven into things is, so we are told, something widely different from what subsequent analysis recovers out of them.

Those who hold this view do not see that it is impossible to escape from thought. I cannot get outside thought when I want to observe it. We should never forget that the distinction between thought which goes on unconsciously and thought which is consciously analysed, is a purely external one and irrelevant to our discussion. I do not in any way alter a thing by making it an object of thought. I can well imagine that a being with quite different sense-organs, and with a differently constructed intelligence, would have a very different idea of a horse from mine, but I cannot think that my own thought becomes different because I make it an object of knowledge. I myself observe my own processes. We are not talking here of how my thought-processes appear to an intelligence different from mine, but how they appear to me. In any case, the idea which another mind forms of my thought cannot be truer than the one which I form myself. Only if the thought-processes were not my own, but the activity of a being quite different from me, could I maintain that, notwithstanding my forming a definite idea of these thought-processes, their real nature was beyond my comprehension.

So far, there is not the slightest reason why I should regard my thought from any other point of view than my own. I contemplate the rest of the world by means of thought. How should I make of my thought an exception?

I think I have given sufficient reasons for making thought the starting-point for my theory of the world. When Archimedes had discovered the lever, he thought he could lift the whole cosmos out of its hinges, if only he could find a point of support for his instrument. He needed a point which was self-supporting. In thought we have a principle which is self-subsisting. Let us try, therefore, to understand the world starting with thought as our basis. Thought can be grasped by thought. The question is whether by thought we can also grasp something other than thought.

I have so far spoken of thought without taking any account of its vehicle, the human consciousness. Most present-day philosophers would object that, before there can be thought, there must be consciousness. Hence we ought to start, not from thought, but from consciousness. There is no thought, they say without consciousness. In reply I would urge that, in order to clear up the relation between thought and consciousness, I must think about it. Hence I presuppose thought. One might, it is true, retort that, though a philosopher who wishes to understand consciousness, naturally makes use of thought, and so far presupposes it, in the ordinary course of life thought arises within consciousness and therefore presupposes that. Were this answer given to the world-creator, when he was about to create thought, it would, without doubt, be to the point. Thought cannot, of course, come into being before consciousness. The philosopher, however, is not concerned with the creation of the world, but with the understanding of it. Hence he is in search of the starting-point, not for creation, but for the understanding of the world. It seems to me very strange that philosophers are reproached for troubling themselves, above all, about the correctness of their principles, instead of turning straight to the objects which they seek to understand. The world-creator had above all to know how to find a vehicle for thought; the philosopher must seek a firm basis for the understanding of what is given. What does it help us to start with consciousness and make it an object of thought, if we have not first inquired how far it is possible at all to gain any knowledge of things by thought?

We must first consider thought quite impartially without relation to a thinking subject or to an object of thought. For subject and object are both concepts constructed by thought. There is no denying that thought must be understood before anything else can be understood. Whoever denies this, fails to realise that man is not the first link in the chain of creation but the last. Hence, in order to explain the world by means of concepts, we cannot start from the elements of existence which came first in time, but we must begin with those which are nearest and most intimately connected with us. We cannot, with a leap, transport ourselves to the beginning of the world, in order to begin our analysis there, but we must start from the present and see whether we cannot advance from the later to the earlier. As long as Geology fabled fantastic revolutions to account for the present state of the earth, it groped in darkness. It was only when it began to study the processes at present at work on the earth, and from these to argue back to the past, that it gained a firm foundation. As long as Philosophy assumes all sorts of principles, such as atom, motion, matter, will, the unconscious, it will hang in the air. The philosopher can reach his goal only if he adopts that which is last in time as first in his theory. This absolutely last in the world-process is thought.

There are people who say it is impossible to ascertain with certainty whether thought is right or wrong, and that, so far, our starting-point is a doubtful one. It would be just as intelligent to raise doubts as to whether a tree is in itself right or wrong. Thought is a fact, and it is meaningless to speak of the truth or falsity of a fact. I can, at most, be in doubt as to whether thought is rightly employed, just as I can doubt whether a certain tree supplies wood adapted to the making of this or that useful object. It is just the purpose of this book to show how far the application of thought to the world is right or wrong. I can understand anyone doubting whether, by means of thought, we can gain any knowledge of the world, but it is unintelligible to me how anyone can doubt that thought in itself is right.

ADDITION TO THE REVISED EDITION (1918).

In the preceding discussion I have pointed out the importance of the difference between thinking and all other activities of mind. This difference is a fact which is patent to genuinely unprejudiced observation. An observer who does not try to see the facts without preconception will be tempted to bring against my argumentation such objections as these: When I think about a rose, there is involved nothing more than a relation of my "I" to the rose, just as when I feel the beauty of the rose. There subsists a relation between "I" and object in thinking precisely as there does, *e.g.*, in feeling or perceiving. Those who urge this objection fail to bear in mind that it is only in the activity of thinking that the "I," or Ego, knows itself to be identical, right into all the ramifications of the activity, with that which does the thinking. Of no other activity of mind can we say the same. For example, in a feeling of pleasure it is easy for a really careful observer to discriminate between the extent to which the Ego knows itself to be identical with what is active in the feeling, and the extent to which there is something passive in the Ego, so that the pleasure is merely something which happens to the Ego. The same applies to the other mental activities. The main thing is not to confuse the "having of images" with the elaboration of ideas by thinking. Images may appear in the mind dream-wise, like vague intimations. But this is not thinking. True, someone might now urge: If this is what you mean by "thinking," then your thinking contains willing, and you have to do, not with mere thinking, but with the will to think. However, this would justify us only in saying: Genuine thinking must always be willed thinking. But this is quite irrelevant to the characterisation of thinking as this has been given in the preceding discussion. Let it be granted that the nature of thinking necessarily implies its being willed, the point which matters is that nothing is willed which, in being carried out, fails to appear to the Ego as an activity completely its own and under its own supervision. Indeed, we must say that thinking appears to the observer as through and through willed, precisely because of its nature as above defined. If we genuinely try to master all the facts which are relevant to a judgment about the nature of thinking, we cannot fail to observe that, as a mental activity, thinking has the unique character which is here in question.

A reader of whose powers the author of this book has a very high opinion, has objected that it is impossible to speak about thinking as we are here doing, because the supposed observation of active thinking is nothing but an illusion. In reality, what is observed is only the results of an unconscious activity which lies at the basis of thinking. It is only because, and just because, this unconscious activity escapes observation, that the deceptive appearance of the self-existence of the observed thinking arises, just as when an illumination by means of a rapid succession of electric sparks makes us believe that we see a movement. This objection, likewise, rests solely on an inaccurate view of the facts. The objection ignores that it is the Ego itself which, identical with the thinking, observes from within its own activity. The Ego would have to stand outside the thinking in order to suffer the sort of deception which is caused by an illumination with a rapid succession of electric sparks. One might say rather that to indulge in such an analogy is to deceive oneself wilfully, just as if someone, seeing a moving light, were obstinately to affirm that it is being freshly lit by an unknown hand at every point where it appears. No, whoever is bent on seeing in thought anything else than an activity produced—and observable by—the Ego has first to shut his eyes to the plain facts that are there for the looking, in order then to invent a hypothetical activity as the basis of thinking. If he does not wilfully blind himself, he must recognise that all these "hypothetical additions" to thinking take him away from its real nature. Unprejudiced observation shows that nothing is to be counted as belonging to the nature of thinking except what is found in thinking itself. It is impossible to discover the cause of thinking by going outside the realm of thought.

IV

THE WORLD AS PERCEPT

The products of thinking are concepts and ideas. What a concept is cannot be expressed in words. Words can do no more than draw our attention to the fact that we have concepts. When someone perceives a tree, the perception acts as a stimulus for thought. Thus an ideal element is added to the perceived object, and the perceiver regards the object and its ideal complement as belonging together. When the object disappears from the field of his perception, the ideal counterpart alone remains. This latter is the concept of the object. The wider the range of our experience, the larger becomes the number of our concepts. Moreover, concepts are not by any means found in isolation one from the other. They combine to form an ordered and systematic whole. The concept "organism," *e.g.*, combines with those of "development according to law," "growth," and others. Other concepts based on particular objects fuse completely with one another. All concepts formed from particular lions fuse in the universal concept "lion." In this way, all the separate concepts combine to form a closed, conceptual system within which each has its special place. Ideas do not differ qualitatively from concepts. They are but fuller, more saturated, more comprehensive concepts. I attach special importance to the necessity of bearing in mind, here, that I make thought my starting-point, and not concepts and ideas which are first gained by means of thought. These latter presuppose thought. My remarks regarding the self-dependent, self-sufficient character of thought cannot, therefore, be simply transferred to concepts. (I make special mention of this, because it is here that I differ from Hegel, who regards the concept as something primary and ultimate.)

Concepts cannot be derived from perception. This is apparent from the fact that, as man grows up, he slowly and gradually builds up the concepts corresponding to the objects which surround him. Concepts are added to perception.

A philosopher, widely read at the present day (Herbert Spencer), describes the mental process which we perform upon perception as follows: "If, when walking through the fields some day in September, you hear a rustle a few yards in advance, and on observing the ditch-side where it occurs, see the herbage agitated, you will probably turn towards the spot to learn by what this sound and motion are produced. As you approach there flutters into the ditch a partridge; on seeing which your curiosity is satisfied—you have what you call an explanation of the appearances. The explanation, mark, amounts to this—that whereas throughout life you have had countless experiences of disturbance among small stationary bodies, accompanying the movement of other bodies among them, and have generalised the relation between such disturbances and such movements, you consider this particular disturbance explained on finding it to present an instance of the like relation" (*First Principles*, Part I, par. 23). A closer analysis leads to a very different description from that here given. When I hear a noise, my first demand is for the concept which fits this percept. Without this concept, the noise is to me a mere noise. Whoever does not reflect further, hears just the noise and is satisfied with that. But my thought makes it clear to me that the noise is to be regarded as an effect. Thus it is only when I combine the concept of effect with the percept of a noise that I am led to go beyond the particular percept and seek for its cause. The concept of "effect" calls up that of "cause," and my next step is to look for the agent, which I find, say, in a partridge. But these concepts, cause and effect, can never be gained through mere perception, however many instances we bring under review. Perception evokes thought, and it is this which shows me how to link separate experiences together.

If one demands of a "strictly objective science" that it should take its data from perception alone, one must demand also that it abandon all thought. For thought, by its very nature, transcends the objects of perception.

It is time now to pass from thought to the thinker. For it is through the thinker that thought and perception are combined. The human mind is the stage on which concept and percept meet and are linked to one another. In saying this, we already characterise this (human) consciousness. It mediates between thought and perception. In perception the object appears as given, in thought the mind seems to itself to be active. It regards the thing as object and itself as the thinking subject. When thought is directed upon the perceptual world we have consciousness of objects; when it is directed upon itself we have self-consciousness. Human consciousness must, of necessity, be at the same time self-consciousness, because it is a consciousness which thinks. For, when thought contemplates its own activity it makes an object for study of its own essential nature, it makes an object of itself as subject.

It is important to note here that it is only by means of thinking that I am able to determine myself as subject and contrast myself with objects. Therefore thinking must never be regarded as a merely subjective activity. Thinking transcends the distinction of subject and object. It produces these two concepts just as it produces all others. When, therefore, I, as thinking subject, refer a concept to an object, we must not regard this reference as something purely subjective. It is not the subject, but thought, which makes the reference. The subject does not think because it is a subject, rather it conceives itself to be a subject because it can think. The activity of consciousness, in so far as it thinks, is thus not merely subjective. Rather it is neither subjective nor objective; it transcends both these concepts. I ought never to say that I, as an individual subject, think, but rather that I, as subject, exist myself by the grace of thought. Thought thus takes me out of myself and relates me to objects. At the same time it separates me from them, inasmuch as I, as subject, am set over against the objects.

It is just this which constitutes the double nature of man. His thought embraces himself and the rest of the world. But by this same act of thought he determines himself also as an individual, in contrast with the objective world.

We must next ask ourselves how the other element, which we have so far simply called the perceptual object and which comes, in consciousness, into contact with thought, enters into thought at all?

In order to answer this question, we must eliminate from the field of consciousness everything which has been imported by thought. For, at any moment, the content of consciousness is always shot through with concepts in the most various ways.

Let us assume that a being with fully developed human intelligence originated out of nothing and confronted the world. All that it there perceived before its thought began to act would be the pure content of perception. The world so far would appear to this being as a mere chaotic aggregate of sense-data, colours, sounds, sensations of pressure, of warmth, of taste, of smell, and, lastly, feelings of pleasure and pain. This mass constitutes the world of pure unthinking perception. Over against it stands thought, ready to begin its activity as soon as it can find a point of attack. Experience shows that the opportunity is not long in coming. Thought is able to draw threads from one sense-datum to another. It brings definite concepts to bear on these data and thus establishes a relation between them. We have seen above how a noise which we hear is connected with another content by our identifying the first as the effect of the second.

If now we recollect that the activity of thought is on no account to be considered as merely subjective, then we shall not be tempted to believe that the relations thus established by thought have merely subjective validity.

Our next task is to discover by means of thought what relation the above-mentioned immediate sense-data have to the conscious subject.

The ambiguity of current speech makes it advisable for me to come to an agreement with my readers concerning the meaning of a word which I shall have to employ in what follows. I shall apply the name "percepts" to the immediate sense-data enumerated above, in so far as the subject consciously apprehends them. It is, then, not the process of perception, but the object of this process which I call the "percept."

I reject the term "sensation," because this has a definite meaning in Physiology which is narrower than that of my term "percept." I can speak of feeling as a percept, but not as a sensation in the physiological sense of the term. Before I can have cognisance of my feeling it must become a percept for me. The manner in which, through observation, we gain knowledge of our thought-processes is such that when we first begin to notice thought, it too may be called a percept.

The unreflective man regards his percepts, such as they appear to his immediate apprehension, as things having a wholly independent existence. When he sees a tree he believes that it stands in the form which he sees, with the colours of all its parts, etc., there on the spot towards which his gaze is directed. When the same man sees the sun in the morning appear as a disc on the horizon, and follows the course of this disc, he believes that the phenomenon exists and occurs (by itself) exactly as he perceives it. To this belief he clings until he meets with further percepts which contradict his former ones. The child who has as yet had no experience of distance grasps at the moon, and does not correct its first impression as to the real distance until a second percept contradicts the first. Every extension of the circle of my percepts compels me to correct my picture of the world. We see this in everyday life, as well as in the mental development of mankind. The picture which the ancients made for themselves of the relation of the earth to the sun and other heavenly bodies, had to be replaced by another when Copernicus found that it contradicted percepts which in those early days were unknown. A man who had been born blind said, when operated on by Dr. Franz, that the idea of the size of objects which he had formed before his operation by his sense of touch was a very different one. He had to correct his tactual percepts by his visual percepts.

How is it that we are compelled to make these continual corrections in our observations?

A single reflection supplies the answer to this question. When I stand at one end of an avenue, the trees at the other end, away from me, seem smaller and nearer together than those where I stand. But the scene which I perceive changes when I change the place from which I am looking. The exact form in which it presents itself to me is, therefore, dependent on a condition which inheres, not in the object, but in me, the percipient. It is all the same to the avenue where I stand. But the picture of it which I receive depends essentially on my standpoint. In the same way, it makes no difference to the sun and the planetary system that human beings happen to perceive them from the earth; but the picture of the heavens which human beings have is determined by the fact that they inhabit the earth. This dependence of our percepts on our points of observation is the easiest kind of dependence to understand. The matter becomes more difficult when we realise further that our perceptual world is dependent on our bodily and mental organisation. The physicist teaches us that within the space in which we hear a sound there are vibrations of the air, and that there are vibrations also in the particles of the body which we regard as the cause of the sound. These vibrations are perceived as sounds only if we have normally constructed ears. Without them the whole world would be for us for ever silent. Again, the physiologist teaches us that there are men who perceive nothing of the wonderful display of colours which surrounds us. In their world there are only degrees of light and dark. Others are blind only to one colour, *e.g.*, red. Their world lacks this colour tone, and hence it is actually a different one from that of the average man. I should like to call the dependence of my perceptual world on my point of observation "mathematical," and its dependence on my organisation "qualitative." The former determines proportions of size and mutual distances of my percepts, the latter their quality. The fact that I see a red surface as red—this qualitative determination—depends on the structure of my eye.

My percepts, then, are in the first instance subjective. The recognition of the subjective character of our percepts may easily lead us to doubt whether there is any objective basis for them at all. When we know that a percept, *e.g.*, that of a red colour or of a certain tone, is not possible without a specific structure of our organism, we may easily be led to believe that it has no being at all apart from our subjective organisation, that it has no kind of existence apart from the act of perceiving of which it is the object. The classical representative of this theory is George Berkeley, who held that from the moment we realise the importance of a subject for perception, we are no longer able to believe in the existence of a world apart from a conscious mind. "Some truths there are so near and obvious to the mind that man need only open his eyes to see them. Such I take this important one to be, viz., that all the choir of heaven and the furniture of the earth—in a word, all those bodies which compose the mighty frame of the world—have not any subsistence without a mind; that their being is to be perceived or known; that consequently, so long as they are not actually perceived by me, or do not exist in my mind or that of any other created spirit, they must either have no existence at all or else subsist in the mind of some Eternal Spirit" (Berkeley, *Of the Principles of Human Knowledge*, Part I, Section 6).

On this view, when we take away the act of perceiving, nothing remains of the percept. There is no colour when none is seen, no sound when none is heard. Extension, form, and motion exist as little as colour and sound apart from the act of perception. We never perceive bare extension or shape. These are always joined with colour or some other quality, which are undoubtedly dependent on the subject. If these latter disappear when we cease to perceive, the former, being connected with them, must disappear likewise.

If it is urged that, even though figure, colour, sound, etc., have no existence except in the act of perception, yet there must be things which exist apart from perception and which are similar to the percepts in our minds, then the view we have mentioned would answer, that a colour can be similar only to a colour, a figure to a figure. Our percepts can be similar only to our percepts and to nothing else. Even what we call a thing is nothing but a collection of percepts which are connected in a definite way. If I strip a table of its shape, extension, colour, etc.—in short, of all that is merely my percepts—then nothing remains over. If we follow this view to its logical conclusion, we are led to the assertion that the objects of my perceptions exist only through me, and only in as far as, and as long as, I perceive them. They disappear with my perceiving and have no meaning apart from it. Apart from my percepts I know of no objects and cannot know of any.

No objection can be made to this assertion as long as we take into account merely the general fact that the percept is determined in part by the organisation of the subject. The matter would be far otherwise if we were in a position to say what part exactly is played by our perceiving in the occurrence of a percept. We should know then what happens to a percept whilst it is being perceived, and we should also be able to determine what character it must possess before it comes to be perceived.

This leads us to turn our attention from the object of a perception to the subject of it. I am aware not only of other things but also of myself. The content of my perception of myself consists, in the first instance, in that I am something stable in contrast with the ever coming and going flux of percepts. The awareness of myself accompanies in my consciousness the awareness of all other percepts. When I am absorbed in the perception of a given object I am, for the time being, aware only of this object. Next I become aware also of myself. I am then conscious, not only of the object, but also of my Self as opposed to and observing the object. I do not merely see a tree, I know also that it is I who see it. I know, moreover, that some process takes place in me when I observe a tree. When the tree disappears from my field of vision, an after-effect of this process remains, viz., an image of the tree. This image has become associated with my Self during my perception. My Self has become enriched; to its content a new element has been added. This element I call my idea of the tree. I should never have occasion to talk of ideas, were I not aware of my own Self. Percepts would come and go; I should let them slip by. It is only because I am aware of my Self, and observe that with each perception the content of the Self is changed, that I am compelled to connect the perception of the object with the changes in the content of my Self, and to speak of having an idea.

That I have ideas is in the same sense matter of observation to me as that other objects have colour, sound, etc. I am now also able to distinguish these other objects, which stand over against me, by the name of the outer world, whereas the contents of my perception of my Self form my inner world. The failure to recognise the true relation between idea and object has led to the greatest misunderstandings in modern philosophy. The fact that I perceive a change in myself, that my Self undergoes a modification, has been thrust into the foreground, whilst the object which causes these modifications is altogether ignored. In consequence it has been said that we perceive, not objects, but only our ideas. I know, so it is said, nothing of the table in itself, which is the object of my perception, but only of the changes which occur within me when I perceive a table. This theory should not be confused with the Berkeleyan theory mentioned above. Berkeley maintains the subjective nature of my perceptual contents, but he does not say that I can know only my own ideas. He limits my knowledge to my ideas because, on his view, there are no objects other than ideas. What I perceive as a table no longer exists, according to Berkeley, when I cease to look at it. This is why Berkeley holds that our percepts are created directly by the omnipotence of God. I see a table because God causes this percept in me. For Berkeley, therefore, nothing is real except God and human spirits. What we call the "world" exists only in spirits. What the naïve man calls the outer world, or material nature, is for Berkeley non-existent. This theory is confronted by the now predominant Kantian view which limits our knowledge of the world to our ideas, not because of any conviction that nothing beyond these ideas exists, but because it holds that we are so organised that we can have knowledge only of the changes within our own selves, not of the things-in-themselves which are the causes of these changes. This view concludes from the fact that I know only my own ideas, not that there is no reality independent of them, but only that the subject cannot have direct knowledge of such reality. The mind can merely "through the medium of its subjective thoughts imagine it, conceive it, know it, or perhaps also fail to know it" (O. Liebmann, *Zur Analysis der Wirklichkeit*, p. 28). Kantians believe that their principles are absolutely certain, indeed immediately evident, without any proof. "The most fundamental principle which the philosopher must begin by grasping clearly, consists in the recognition that our knowledge, in the first instance, does not extend beyond our ideas. Our ideas are all that we immediately have and experience, and just because we have immediate experience of them the most radical doubt cannot rob us of this knowledge. On the other hand, the knowledge which transcends my ideas—taking ideas here in the widest possible sense, so as to include all psychical processes—is not proof against doubt. Hence, at the very beginning of all philosophy we must explicitly set down all knowledge which transcends ideas as open to doubt." These are the opening sentences of Volkelt's book on *Kant's Theory of Knowledge*. What is here put forward as an immediate and self-evident truth is, in reality, the conclusion of a piece of argument which runs as follows. Naïve common sense believes that things, just as we perceive them, exist also outside our minds. Physics, Physiology, and Psychology, however, teach us that our percepts are dependent on our organisation, and that therefore we cannot know anything about external objects except what our organisation transmits to us. The objects which we perceive are thus modifications of our organisation, not things-in-themselves. This line of thought has, in fact, been characterised by Ed. von Hartmann as the one which leads necessarily to the conviction that we can have direct knowledge only of our own ideas (*cp.* his *Grundproblem der Erkenntnistheorie,* pp. 16–40). Because outside our organisms we find vibrations of particles and of air, which are perceived by us as sounds, it is concluded that what we call sound is nothing more than a subjective reaction of our organisms to these motions in the external world. Similarly, colour and heat are inferred to be merely modifications of our organisms. And, further, these two kinds of percepts are held to be the effects of processes in the external world which are utterly different from what we experience as heat or as colour. When these processes stimulate the nerves in the skin of my body, I perceive heat; when they stimulate the optical nerve I perceive light and colour. Light, colour, and heat, then, are the reactions of my sensory nerves to external stimuli. Similarly, the sense of touch reveals to me, not the objects of the outer world, but only states of my own body. The physicist holds that bodies are composed of infinitely small particles called molecules, and that these molecules are not in direct contact with one another, but have definite intervals between them. Between them, therefore, is empty space. Across this space they act on one another by attraction and repulsion. If I put my hand on a body, the molecules of my hand by no means touch those of the body directly, but there remains a certain distance between body and hand, and what I experience as the body's resistance is nothing but the effect of the force of repulsion which its molecules exert on my hand. I am absolutely external to the body and experience only its effects on my organism.

The theory of the so-called Specific Nervous Energy, which has been advanced by J. Müller, supplements these speculations. It asserts that each sense has the peculiarity that it reacts to all external stimuli in only one definite way. If the optic nerve is stimulated, light sensations result, irrespective of whether the stimulation is due to what we call light, or to mechanical pressure, or an electrical current. On the other hand, the same external stimulus applied to different senses gives rise to different sensations. The conclusion from these facts seems to be, that our sense-organs can give us knowledge only of what occurs in themselves, but not of the external world. They determine our percepts, each according to its own nature.

Physiology shows, further, that there can be no direct knowledge even of the effects which objects produce on our sense-organs. Through his study of the processes which occur in our own bodies, the physiologist finds that, even in the sense-organs, the effects of the external process are modified in the most diverse ways. We can see this most clearly in the case of eye and ear. Both are very complicated organs which modify the external stimulus considerably, before they conduct it to the corresponding nerve. From the peripheral end of the nerve the modified stimulus is then conducted to the brain. Here the central organs must in turn be stimulated. The conclusion is, therefore, drawn that the external process undergoes a series of transformations before it reaches consciousness. The brain processes are connected by so many intermediate links with the external stimuli, that any similarity between them is out of the question. What the brain ultimately transmits to the soul is neither external processes, nor processes in the sense-organs, but only such as occur in the brain. But even these are not apprehended immediately by the soul. What we finally have in consciousness are not brain processes at all, but sensations. My sensation of red has absolutely no similarity with the process which occurs in the brain when I sense red. The sensation, again, occurs as an effect in the mind, and the brain process is only its cause. This is why Hartmann (*Grundproblem der Erkenntnistheorie*, p. 37) says, "What the subject experiences is therefore only modifications of his own psychical states and nothing else." However, when I have sensations, they are very far as yet from being grouped in those complexes which I perceive as "things." Only single sensations can be transmitted to me by the brain. The sensations of hardness and softness are transmitted to me by the organ of touch, those of colour and light by the organ of sight. Yet all these are found united in one object. This unification must, therefore, be brought about by the soul itself; that is, the soul constructs things out of the separate sensations which the brain conveys to it. My brain conveys to me singly, and by widely different paths, the visual, tactual, and auditory sensations which the soul then combines into the idea of a trumpet. Thus, what is really the result of a process (*i.e.*, the idea of a trumpet), is for my consciousness the primary datum. In this result nothing can any longer be found of what exists outside of me and originally stimulated my sense-organs. The external object is lost entirely on the way to the brain and through the brain to the soul.

It would be hard to find in the history of human speculation another edifice of thought which has been built up with greater ingenuity, and which yet, on closer analysis, collapses into nothing. Let us look a little closer at the way it has been constructed. The theory starts with what is given in naïve consciousness, *i.e.*, with things as perceived. It proceeds to show that none of the qualities which we find in these things would exist for us, had we no sense-organs. No eye—no colour. Therefore, the colour is not, as yet, present in the stimulus which affects the eye. It arises first through the interaction of the eye and the object. The latter is, therefore, colourless. But neither is the colour in the eye, for in the eye there is only a chemical, or physical, process which is first conducted by the optic nerve to the brain, and there initiates another process. Even this is not yet the colour. That is only produced in the soul by means of the brain process. Even then it does not yet appear in consciousness, but is first referred by the soul to a body in the external world. There I finally perceive it, as a quality of this body. We have travelled in a complete circle. We are conscious of a coloured object. That is the starting-point. Here thought begins its construction. If I had no eye, the object would be, for me, colourless. I cannot, therefore, attribute the colour to the object. I must look for it elsewhere. I look for it, first, in the eye—in vain; in the nerve—in vain; in the brain—in vain once more; in the soul—here I find it indeed, but not attached to the object. I recover the coloured body only on returning to my starting-point. The circle is completed. The theory leads me to identify what the naïve man regards as existing outside of him, as really a product of my mind.

As long as one stops here everything seems to fit beautifully. But we must go over the argument once more from the beginning. Hitherto I have used, as my starting-point, the object, *i.e.*, the external percept of which up to now, from my naïve standpoint, I had a totally wrong conception. I thought that the percept, just as I perceive it, had objective existence. But now I observe that it disappears with my act of perception, that it is only a modification of my mental state. Have I, then, any right at all to start from it in my arguments? Can I say of it that it acts on my soul? I must henceforth treat the table of which formerly I believed that it acted on me, and produced an idea of itself in me, as itself an idea. But from this it follows logically that my sense-organs, and the processes in them are also merely subjective. I have no right to talk of a real eye but only of my idea of an eye. Exactly the same is true of the nerve paths, and the brain processes, and even of the process in the soul itself, through which things are supposed to be constructed out of the chaos of diverse sensations. If assuming the truth of the first circle of argumentation, I run through the steps of my cognitive activity once more, the latter reveals itself as a tissue of ideas which, as such, cannot act on one another. I cannot say that my idea of the object acts on my idea of the eye, and that from this interaction results my idea of colour. But it is necessary that I should say this. For as soon as I see clearly that my sense-organs and their activity, my nerve- and soul-processes, can also be known to me only through perception, the argument which I have outlined reveals itself in its full absurdity. It is quite true that I can have no percept without the corresponding sense-organ. But just as little can I be aware of a sense-organ without perception. From the percept of a table I can pass to the eye which sees it, or the nerves in the skin which touches it, but what takes place in these I can, in turn, learn only from perception. And then I soon perceive that there is no trace of similarity between the process which takes place in the eye and the colour which I see. I cannot get rid of colour sensations by pointing to the process which takes place in the eye whilst I perceive a colour. No more can I re-discover the colour in the nerve- or brain-processes. I only add a new percept, localised within the organism, to the first percept which the naïve man localises outside of his organism. I only pass from one percept to another.

Moreover, there is a break in the whole argument. I can follow the processes in my organism up to those in my brain, even though my assumptions become more and more hypothetical as I approach the central processes of the brain. The method of external observation ceases with the process in my brain, more particularly with the process which I should observe, if I could treat the brain with the instruments and methods of Physics and Chemistry. The method of internal observation, or introspection, begins with the sensations, and includes the construction of things out of the material of sense-data. At the point of transition from brain process to sensation, there is a break in the sequence of observation.

The theory which I have here described, and which calls itself Critical Idealism, in contrast to the standpoint of naïve common sense which it calls Naïve Realism, makes the mistake of characterising one group of percepts as ideas, whilst taking another group in the very same sense as the Naïve Realism which it apparently refutes. It establishes the ideal character of percepts by accepting naïvely, as objectively valid facts, the percepts connected with one's own body; and, in addition, it fails to see that it confuses two spheres of observation, between which it can find no connecting link.

Critical Idealism can refute Naïve Realism only by itself assuming, in naïve-realistic fashion, that one's own organism has objective existence. As soon as the Idealist realises that the percepts connected with his own organism stand on exactly the same footing as those which Naïve Realism assumes to have objective existence, he can no longer use the former as a safe foundation for his theory. He would, to be consistent, have to regard his own organism also as a mere complex of ideas. But this removes the possibility of regarding the content of the perceptual world as a product of the mind's organisation. One would have to assume that the idea "colour" was only a modification of the idea "eye." So-called Critical Idealism can be established only by borrowing the assumptions of Naïve Realism. The apparent refutation of the latter is achieved only by uncritically accepting its own assumptions as valid in another sphere.

This much, then, is certain: Analysis within the world of percepts cannot establish Critical Idealism, and, consequently, cannot strip percepts of their objective character.

Still less is it legitimate to represent the principle that "the perceptual world is my idea" as self-evident and needing no proof. Schopenhauer begins his chief work, *The World as Will and Idea*, with the words: "The world is my idea—this is a truth which holds good for everything that lives and knows, though man alone can bring it into reflective and abstract consciousness. If he really does this, he has attained to philosophical wisdom. It then becomes clear and certain to him that what he knows is not a sun and an earth, but only an eye that sees a sun, a hand that feels an earth; that the world which surrounds him is there only in idea, *i.e.*, only in relation to something else, the consciousness which is himself. If any truth can be asserted *a priori*, it is this: for it is the expression of the most general form of all possible and thinkable experience, a form which is more general than time, or space, or causality, for they all presuppose it ..." (*The World as Will and Idea*, Book I, par. 1). This whole theory is wrecked by the fact, already mentioned above, that the eyes and the hand are just as much percepts as the sun and the earth. Using Schopenhauer's vocabulary in his own sense, I might maintain against him that my eye which sees the sun, and my hand which feels the earth, are my ideas just like the sun and the earth themselves. That, put in this way, the whole theory cancels itself, is clear without further argument. For only my real eye and my real hand, but not my ideas "eye" and "hand," could own the ideas "sun" and "earth" as modifications. Yet it is only in terms of these ideas that Critical Idealism has the right to speak.

Critical Idealism is totally unable to gain an insight unto the relation of percept to idea. It cannot make the separation, mentioned on p. 58, between what happens to the percept in the process of perception and what must be inherent in it prior to perception. We must therefore attempt this problem in another way.

v

OUR KNOWLEDGE OF THE WORLD

From the foregoing considerations it follows that it is impossible to prove, by analysis of the content of our perceptions, that our percepts are ideas. This is supposed to be proved by showing that, if the process of perceiving takes place in the way in which we conceive it in accordance with the naïve-realistic assumptions concerning the psychological and physiological constitution of human individuals, then we have to do, not with things themselves, but merely with our ideas of things. Now, if Naïve Realism, when consistently thought out, leads to results which directly contradict its presuppositions, then these presuppositions must be discarded as unsuitable for the foundation of a theory of the world. In any case, it is inadmissible to reject the presuppositions and yet accept the consequences, as the Critical Idealist does who bases his assertion that the world is my idea on the line of argument indicated above. (Eduard von Hartmann gives in his work *Das Grundproblem der Erkenntnistheorie* a full account of this line of argument.)

The truth of Critical Idealism is one thing, the persuasiveness of its proofs another. How it stands with the former, will appear later in the course of our argument, but the persuasiveness of its proofs is nil. If one builds a house, and the ground floor collapses whilst the first floor is being built, then the first floor collapses too. Naïve Realism and Critical Idealism are related to one another like the ground floor to the first floor in this simile.

For one who holds that the whole perceptual world is only an ideal world, and, moreover, the effect of things unknown to him acting on his soul, the real problem of knowledge is naturally concerned, not with the ideas present only in the soul, but with the things which lie outside his consciousness, and which are independent of him. He asks, How much can we learn about them indirectly, seeing that we cannot observe them directly? From this point of view, he is concerned, not with the connection of his conscious percepts with one another, but with their causes which transcend his consciousness and exist independently of him, whereas the percepts, on his view, disappear as soon as he turns his sense-organs away from the things themselves. Our consciousness, on this view, works like a mirror from which the pictures of definite things disappear the very moment its reflecting surface is not turned towards them. If, now, we do not see the things themselves, but only their reflections, we must obtain knowledge of the nature of the former indirectly by drawing conclusions from the character of the latter. The whole of modern science adopts this point of view, when it uses percepts only as a means of obtaining information about the motions of matter which lie behind them, and which alone really "are." If the philosopher, as Critical Idealist, admits real existence at all, then his sole aim is to gain knowledge of this real existence indirectly by means of his ideas. His interest ignores the subjective world of ideas, and pursues instead the causes of these ideas.

The Critical Idealist can, however, go even further and say, I am confined to the world of my own ideas and cannot escape from it. If I conceive a thing beyond my ideas, this concept, once more, is nothing but my idea. An Idealist of this type will either deny the thing-in-itself entirely or, at any rate, assert that it has no significance for human minds, *i.e.*, that it is as good as non-existent since we can know nothing of it.

To this kind of Critical Idealist the whole world seems a chaotic dream, in the face of which all striving for knowledge is simply meaningless. For him there can be only two sorts of men: (1) victims of the illusion that the dreams they have woven themselves are real things, and (2) wise men who see through the nothingness of this dream world, and who gradually lose all desire to trouble themselves further about it. From this point of view, even one's own personality may become a mere dream phantom. Just as during sleep there appears among my dream-images an image of myself, so in waking consciousness the idea of my own Self is added to the idea of the outer world. I have then given to me in consciousness, not my real Self, but only my idea of my Self. Whoever denies that things exist, or, at least, that we can know anything of them, must also deny the existence, respectively the knowledge, of one's own personality. This is how the Critical Idealist comes to maintain that "All reality transforms itself into a wonderful dream, without a life which is the object of the dream, and without a mind which has the dream; into a dream which is nothing but a dream of itself." (*Cp.* Fichte, *Die Bestimmung des Menschen*.)

Whether he who believes that he recognises immediate experience to be a dream, postulates nothing behind this dream, or whether he relates his ideas to actual things, is immaterial. In both cases life itself must lose all scientific interest for him. However, whereas for those who believe that the whole of accessible reality is exhausted in dreams, all science is an absurdity, for those who feel compelled to argue from ideas to things, science consists in studying these things-in-themselves. The first of these theories of the world may be called Absolute Illusionism, the second is called Transcendental Realism[1] by its most rigorously logical exponent, Eduard von Hartmann.

These two points of view have this in common with Naïve Realism, that they seek to gain a footing in the world by means of an analysis of percepts. Within this sphere, however, they are unable to find any stable point.

One of the most important questions for an adherent of Transcendental Realism would have to be, how the Ego constructs the world of ideas out of itself. A world of ideas which was given to us, and which disappeared as soon as we shut our senses to the external world, might provoke an earnest desire for knowledge, in so far as it was a means for investigating indirectly the world of the self-existing Self. If the things of our experience were "ideas," then our everyday life would be like a dream, and the discovery of the true facts like waking. Even our dream-images interest us as long as we dream and, consequently, do not detect their dream character. But as soon as we wake, we no longer look for the connections of our dream-images among themselves, but rather for the physical, physiological, and psychological processes which underlie them. In the same way, a philosopher who holds the world to be his idea, cannot be interested in the reciprocal relations of the details within the world. If he admits the existence of a real Ego at all, then his question will be, not how one of his ideas is associated with another, but what takes place in the Soul which is independent of these ideas, while a certain train of ideas passes through his consciousness. If I dream that I am drinking wine which makes my throat burn, and then wake up with a fit of coughing (*cp.* Weygandt, *Entstehung der Träume*, 1893) I cease, the moment I wake, to be interested in the dream-experience for its own sake. My attention is now concerned only with the physiological and psychological processes by means of which the irritation which causes me to cough, comes to be symbolically expressed in the dream. Similarly, once the philosopher is convinced that the given world consists of nothing but ideas, his interest is bound to switch from them at once to the soul which is the reality lying behind them. The matter is more serious, however, for the Illusionist who denies the existence of an Ego behind the "ideas," or at least holds this Ego to be unknowable. We might very easily be led to such a view by the reflection that, in contrast to dreaming, there is the waking state in which we have the opportunity to detect our dreams, and to realise the real relations of things, but that there is no state of the self which is related similarly to our waking conscious life. Every adherent of this view fails entirely to see that there is, in fact, something which is to mere perception what our waking experience to our dreams. This something is thought.

The naïve man cannot be charged with failure to perceive this. He accepts life as it is, and regards things as real just as they present themselves to him in experience. The first step, however, which we take beyond this standpoint can be only this, that we ask how thought is related to perception. It makes no difference whether or no the percept, as given to me, has a continuous existence before and after I perceive it. If I want to assert anything whatever about it, I can do so only with the help of thought. When I assert that the world is my idea, I have enunciated the result of an act of thought, and if my thought is not applicable to the world, then my result is false. Between a percept and every kind of judgment about it there intervenes thought.

The reason why, in our discussion about things, we generally overlook the part played by thought, has already been given above (p. 31). It lies in the fact that our attention is concentrated only on the object about which we think, but not at the same time on the thinking itself. The naïve mind, therefore, treats thought as something which has nothing to do with things, but stands altogether aloof from them and makes its theories about them. The theory which the thinker constructs concerning the phenomena of the world is regarded, not as part of the real things, but as existing only in men's heads. The world is complete in itself even without this theory. It is all ready-made and finished with all its substances and forces, and of this ready-made world man makes himself a picture. Whoever thinks thus need only be asked one question. What right have you to declare the world to be complete without thought? Does not the world cause thoughts in the minds of men with the same necessity as it causes the blossoms on plants? Plant a seed in the earth. It puts forth roots and stem, it unfolds into leaves and blossoms. Set the plant before yourselves. It connects itself, in your minds, with a definite concept. Why should this concept belong any less to the whole plant than leaf and blossom? You say the leaves and blossoms exist quite apart from an experiencing subject. The concept appears only when a human being makes an object of the plant. Quite so. But leaves and blossoms also appear on the plant only if there is soil in which the seed can be planted, and light and air in which the blossoms and leaves can unfold. Just so the concept of a plant arises when a thinking being comes into contact with the plant.

It is quite arbitrary to regard the sum of what we experience of a thing through bare perception as a totality, a whole, while that which thought reveals in it is regarded as a mere accretion which has nothing to do with the thing itself. If I am given a rosebud to-day, the percept that offers itself to me is complete only for the moment. If I put the bud into water, I shall to-morrow get a very different picture of my object. If I watch the rosebud without interruption, I shall see to-day's state gradually change into to-morrow's through an infinite number of intermediate stages. The picture which presents itself to me at any one moment is only a chance section out of the continuous process of growth in which the object is engaged. If I do not put the bud into water, a whole series of states, the possibility of which lay in the bud, will not be realised. Similarly, I may be prevented to-morrow from watching the blossom further, and thus carry away an incomplete picture of it.

It would be a quite unscientific and arbitrary judgment which declared of any haphazard appearance of a thing, this is the thing.

To regard the sum of perceptual appearances as the thing is no more legitimate. It might be quite possible for a mind to receive the concept at the same time as, and together with, the percept. To such a mind it would never occur that the concept did not belong to the thing. It would have to ascribe to the concept an existence indivisibly bound up with the thing.

Let me make myself clearer by another example. If I throw a stone horizontally through the air, I perceive it in different places at different times. I connect these places so as to form a line. Mathematics teaches me to distinguish various kinds of lines, one of which is the parabola. I know a parabola to be a line which is produced by a point moving according to a certain well-defined law. If I analyse the conditions under which the stone thrown by me moves, I find that the line of its flight is identical with the line I know as a parabola. That the stone moves exactly in a parabola is a result of the given conditions and follows necessarily from them. The form of the parabola belongs to the whole phenomenon as much as any other feature of it. The hypothetical mind described above which has no need of the roundabout way of thought, would find itself presented, not only with a sequence of visual percepts at different points, but, as part and parcel of these phenomena, also with the parabolic form of the line of flight, which we can add to the phenomenon only by an act of thought.

It is not due to the real objects that they appear to us at first without their conceptual sides, but to our mental organisation. Our whole organisation functions in such a way that in the apprehension of every real thing the relevant elements come to us from two sources, viz., from perception and from thought.

The nature of things is indifferent to the way I am organised for apprehending them. The breach between perception and thought exists only from the moment that I confront objects as spectator. But which elements do, and which do not, belong to the objects, cannot depend on the manner in which I obtain my knowledge of them.

Man is a being with many limitations. First of all, he is a thing among other things. His existence is in space and time. Hence but a limited portion of the total universe can ever be given to him. This limited portion, however, is linked up with other parts on every side both in time and in space. If our existence were so linked with things that every process in the object world were also a process in us, there would be no difference between us and things. Neither would there be any individual objects for us. All processes and events would then pass continuously one into the other. The cosmos would be a unity and a whole complete in itself. The stream of events would nowhere be interrupted. But owing to our limitations we perceive as an individual object what, in truth, is not an individual object at all. Nowhere, *e.g.*, is the particular quality "red" to be found by itself in abstraction. It is surrounded on all sides by other qualities to which it belongs, and without which it could not subsist. For us, however, it is necessary to isolate certain sections of the world and to consider them by themselves. Our eye can seize only single colours one after another out of a manifold colour-complex, our understanding only single concepts out of a connected conceptual system. This isolation is a subjective act, which is due to the fact that we are not identical with the world-process, but are only things among other things.

It is of the greatest importance for us to determine the relation of ourselves, as things, to all other things. The determining of this relation must be distinguished from merely becoming conscious of ourselves. For this self-awareness we depend on perception just as we do for our awareness of any other thing. The perception of myself reveals to me a number of qualities which I combine into an apprehension of my personality as a whole, just as I combine the qualities, yellow, metallic, hard, etc., in the unity "gold." This kind of self-consciousness does not take me beyond the sphere of what belongs to me. Hence it must be distinguished from the determination of myself by thought. Just as I determine by thought the place of any single percept of the external world in the whole cosmic system, so I fit by an act of thought what I perceive in myself into the order of the world-process. My self-observation restricts me within definite limits, but my thought has nothing to do with these limits. In this sense I am a two-sided being. I am contained within the sphere which I apprehend as that of my personality, but I am also the possessor of an activity which, from a higher standpoint, determines my finite existence. Thought is not individual like sensation and feeling; it is universal. It receives an individual stamp in each separate human being only because it comes to be related to his individual feelings and sensations. By means of these particular colourings of the universal thought, individual men are distinguished from one another. There is only one single concept of "triangle." It is quite immaterial for the content of this concept whether it is in A's consciousness or in B's. It will, however, be grasped by each of the two minds in its own individual way.

This thought conflicts with a common prejudice which is very hard to overcome. The victims of this prejudice are unable to see that the concept of a triangle which my mind grasps is the same as the concept which my neighbour's mind grasps. The naïve man believes himself to be the creator of his concepts. Hence he believes that each person has his private concepts. One of the first things which philosophic thought requires of us is to overcome this prejudice. The one single concept of "triangle" does not split up into many concepts because it is thought by many minds. For the thought of the many is itself a unity.

In thought we have the element which welds each man's special individuality into one whole with the cosmos. In so far as we sense and feel (perceive), we are isolated individuals; in so far as we think, we are the All-One Being which pervades everything. This is the deeper meaning of our two-sided nature. We are conscious of an absolute principle revealing itself in us, a principle which is universal. But we experience it, not as it issues from the centre of the world, but rather at a point on the periphery. Were the former the case, we should know, as soon as ever we became conscious, the solution of the whole world problem. But since we stand at a point on the periphery, and find that our own being is confined within definite limits, we must explore the region which lies beyond our own being with the help of thought, which is the universal cosmic principle manifesting itself in our minds.

The fact that thought, in us, reaches out beyond our separate existence and relates itself to the universal world-order, gives rise to the desire for knowledge in us. Beings without thought do not experience this desire. When they come in contact with other things no questions arise for them. These other things remain external to such beings. But in thinking beings the concept confronts the external thing. It is that part of the thing which we receive not from without, but from within. To assimilate, to unite, the two elements, the inner and the outer, that is the function of knowledge.

The percept, thus, is not something finished and self-contained, but one side only of the total reality. The other side is the concept. The act of cognition is the synthesis of percept and concept. And it is only the union of percept and concept which constitutes the whole thing.

The preceding discussion shows clearly that it is futile to seek for any other common element in the separate things of the world than the ideal content which thinking supplies. All attempts to discover any other principle of unity in the world than this internally coherent ideal content, which we gain for ourselves by the conceptual analysis of our percepts, are bound to fail. Neither a personal God, nor force, nor matter, nor the blind will (of Schopenhauer and Hartmann), can be accepted by us as the universal principle of unity in the world. These principles all belong only to a limited sphere of our experience. Personality we experience only in ourselves, force and matter only in external things. The will, again, can be regarded only as the expression of the activity of our finite personalities. Schopenhauer wants to avoid making "abstract" thought the principle of unity in the world, and seeks instead something which presents itself to him immediately as real. This philosopher holds that we can never solve the riddle of the world so long as we regard it as an "external" world. "In fact, the meaning for which we seek of that world which is present to us only as our idea, or the transition from the world as mere idea of the knowing subject to whatever it may be besides this, would never be found if the investigator himself were nothing more than the pure knowing subject (a winged cherub without a body). But he himself is rooted in that world: he finds himself in it as an individual, that is to say, his knowledge, which is the necessary supporter of the whole world as idea, is yet always given through the medium of a body, whose affections are, as we have shown, the starting-point for the understanding in the perception of that world. His body is, for the pure knowing subject, an idea like every other idea, an object among objects. Its movements and actions are so far known to him in precisely the same way as the changes of all other perceived objects, and would be just as strange and incomprehensible to him if their meaning were not explained for him in an entirely different way.... The body is given in two entirely different ways to the subject of knowledge, who becomes an individual only through his identity with it. It is given as an idea in intelligent perception, as an object among objects and subject to the laws of objects. And it is also given in quite a different way as that which is immediately known to every one, and is signified by the word 'will.' Every true act of his will is also at once and without exception a movement of his body. The act of will and the movement of the body are not two different things objectively known, which the bond of causality unites; they do not stand in the relation of cause and effect; they are one and the same, but they are given in entirely different ways—immediately, and again in perception for the understanding." (*The World as Will and Idea*, Book 2, § 18.) Schopenhauer considers himself entitled by these arguments to hold that the will becomes objectified in the human body. He believes that in the activities of the body he has an immediate experience of reality, of the thing-in-itself in the concrete. Against these arguments we must urge that the activities of our body become known to us only through self-observation, and that, as such, they are in no way superior to other percepts. If we want to know their real nature, we can do so only by means of thought, *i.e.*, by fitting them into the ideal system of our concepts and ideas.

One of the most deeply rooted prejudices of the naïve mind is the opinion that thinking is abstract and empty of any concrete content. At best, we are told, it supplies but an "ideal" counterpart of the unity of the world, but never that unity itself. Whoever holds this view has never made clear to himself what a percept apart from concepts really is. Let us see what this world of bare percepts is. A mere juxtaposition in space, a mere succession in time, a chaos of disconnected particulars—that is what it is. None of these things which come and go on the stage of perception has any connection with any other. The world is a multiplicity of objects without distinctions of value. None plays any greater part in the nexus of the world than any other. In order to realise that this or that fact has a greater importance than another we must go to thought. As long as we do not think, the rudimentary organ of an animal which has no significance in its life, appears equal in value to its more important limbs. The particular facts reveal their meaning, in themselves and in their relations with other parts of the world, only when thought spins its threads from thing to thing. This activity of thinking has always a content. For it is only through a perfectly definite concrete content that I can know why the snail belongs to a lower type of organisation than the lion. The mere appearance, the percept, gives me no content which could inform me as to the degree of perfection of the organisation.

Thought contributes this content to the percept from the world of concepts and ideas. In contrast with the content of perception which is given to us from without, the content of thought appears within our minds. The form in which thought first appears in consciousness we will call "intuition." Intuition is to thoughts what observation is to percepts. Intuition and observation are the sources of our knowledge. An external object which we observe remains unintelligible to us, until the corresponding intuition arises within us which adds to the reality those sides of it which are lacking in the percept. To anyone who is incapable of supplying the relevant intuitions, the full nature of the real remains a sealed book. Just as the colour-blind person sees only differences of brightness without any colour qualities, so the mind which lacks intuition sees only disconnected fragments of percepts.

To explain a thing, to make it intelligible, means nothing else than to place it in the context from which it has been torn by the peculiar organisation of our minds, described above. Nothing can possibly exist cut off from the universe. Hence all isolation of objects has only subjective validity for minds organised like ours. For us the universe is split up into above and below, before and after, cause and effect, object and idea, matter and force, object and subject, etc. The objects which, in observation, appear to us as separate, become combined, bit by bit, through the coherent, unified system of our intuitions. By thought we fuse again into one whole all that perception has separated.

An object presents riddles to our understanding so long as it exists in isolation. But this is an abstraction of our own making and can be unmade again in the world of concepts.

Except through thought and perception nothing is given to us directly. The question now arises as to the interpretation of percepts on our theory. We have learnt that the proof which Critical Idealism offers for the subjective nature of percepts collapses. But the exhibition of the falsity of the proof is not, by itself, sufficient to show that the doctrine itself is an error. Critical Idealism does not base its proof on the absolute nature of thought, but relies on the argument that Naïve Realism, when followed to its logical conclusion, contradicts itself. How does the matter appear when we recognise the absoluteness of thought?

Let us assume that a certain percept, *e.g.*, red, appears in consciousness. To continued observation, the percept shows itself to be connected with other percepts, *e.g.*, a certain figure, temperature, and touch-qualities. This complex of percepts I call an object in the world of sense. I can now ask myself: Over and above the percepts just mentioned, what else is there in the section of space in which they are? I shall then find mechanical, chemical, and other processes in that section of space. I next go further and study the processes which take place between the object and my sense-organs. I shall find oscillations in an elastic medium, the character of which has not the least in common with the percepts from which I started. I get the same result if I trace further the connection between sense-organs and brain. In each of these inquiries I gather new percepts, but the connecting thread which binds all these spatially and temporally separated percepts into one whole, is thought. The air vibrations which carry sound are given to me as percepts just like the sound. Thought alone links all these percepts one to the other and exhibits them in their reciprocal relations. We have no right to say that over and above our immediate percepts there is anything except the ideal nexus of precepts (which thought has to reveal). The relation of the object perceived to the perceiving subject, which relation transcends the bare percept, is therefore purely ideal, *i.e.*, capable of being expressed only through concepts. Only if it were possible to perceive how the object of perception affects the perceiving subject, or, alternatively, only if I could watch the construction of the perceptual complex through the subject, could we speak as modern Physiology, and the Critical Idealism which is based on it, speak. Their theory confuses an ideal relation (that of the object to the subject) with a process of which we could speak only if it were possible to perceive it. The proposition, "No colour without a colour-sensing eye," cannot be taken to mean that the eye produces the colour, but only that an ideal relation, recognisable by thought, subsists between the percept "colour" and the percept "eye."

To empirical science belongs the task of ascertaining how the properties of the eye and those of the colours are related to one another; by means of what structures the organ of sight makes possible the perception of colours, etc. I can trace how one percept succeeds another and how one is related to others in space, and I can formulate these relations in conceptual terms, but I can never perceive how a percept originates out of the non-perceptible. All attempts to seek any relations between percepts other than conceptual relations must of necessity fail.

What then is a percept? This question, asked in this general way, is absurd. A percept appears always as a perfectly determinate, concrete content. This content is immediately given and is completely contained in the given. The only question one can ask concerning the given content is, what it is apart from perception, that is, what it is for thought. The question concerning the "what" of a percept can, therefore, only refer to the conceptual intuition which corresponds to the percept. From this point of view, the problem of the subjectivity of percepts, in the sense in which the Critical Idealists debate it, cannot be raised at all. Only that which is experienced as belonging to the subject can be termed "subjective." To form a link between subject and object is impossible for any real process, in the naïve sense of the word "real," in which it means a process which can be perceived. That is possible only for thought. For us, then, "objective" means that which, for perception, presents itself as external to the perceiving subject. As subject of perception I remain perceptible to myself after the table which now stands before me has disappeared from my field of observation. The perception of the table has produced a modification in me which persists like myself. I preserve an image of the table which now forms part of my

Self. Modern Psychology terms this image a "memory-idea." Now this is the only thing which has any right to be called the idea of the table. For it is the perceptible modification of my own mental state through the presence of the table in my visual field. Moreover, it does not mean a modification in some "Ego-in-itself" behind the perceiving subject, but the modification of the perceiving subject itself. The idea is, therefore, a subjective percept, in contrast with the objective percept which occurs when the object is present in the perceptual field. The false identification of the subjective with this objective percept leads to the misunderstanding of Idealism: The world is my idea.

Our next task must be to define the concept of "idea" more nearly. What we have said about it so far does not give us the concept, but only shows us where in the perceptual field ideas are to be found. The exact concept of "idea" will also make it possible for us to obtain a satisfactory understanding of the relation of idea and object. This will then lead us over the border-line, where the relation of subject to object is brought down from the purely conceptual field of knowledge into concrete individual life. Once we know how we are to conceive the world, it will be an easy task to adapt ourselves to it. Only when we know to what object we are to devote our activity can we put our whole energy into our actions.

ADDITION TO THE REVISED EDITION (1918).

The view which I have here outlined may be regarded as one to which man is led as it were spontaneously, as soon as he begins to reflect about his relation to the world. He then finds himself caught in a system of thoughts which dissolves for him as fast as he frames it. The thoughts which form this system are such that the purely theoretical refutation of them does not exhaust our task. We have to live through them, in order to understand the confusion into which they lead us, and to find the way out. They must figure in any discussion of the relation of man to the world, not for the sake of refuting others whom one believes to be holding mistaken views about this relation, but because it is necessary to understand the confusion in which all first efforts at reflection about such a relation are apt to issue. One needs to learn by experience how to refute oneself with respect to these first reflections. This is the point of view from which the arguments of the preceding chapter are to be understood.

Whoever tries to work out for himself a theory of the relation of man to the world, becomes aware of the fact that he creates this relation, at least in part, by forming ideas about the things and events in the world. In consequence, his attention is deflected from what exists outside in the world and directed towards his inner world, the realm of his ideas. He begins to say to himself, It is impossible for me to stand in relation to any thing or event, unless an idea appears in me. From this fact, once noticed, it is but a step to the theory: all that I experience is only my ideas; of the existence of a world outside I know only in so far as it is an idea in me. With this theory, man abandons the standpoint of Naïve Realism which he occupies prior to all reflection about his relation to the world. So long as he stands there, he believes that he is dealing with real things, but reflection about himself drives him away from this position. Reflection does not reveal to his gaze a real world such as naïve consciousness claims to have before it. Reflection reveals to him only his ideas; they interpose themselves between his own nature and a supposedly real world, such as the naïve point of view confidently affirms. The interposition of the world of ideas prevents man from perceiving any longer such a real world. He must suppose that he is blind to such a reality. Thus arises the concept of a "thing-in-itself" which is inaccessible to knowledge. So long as we consider only the relation to the world into which man appears to enter through the stream of his ideas, we can hardly avoid framing this type of theory. Yet we cannot remain at the point of view of Naïve Realism except at the price of closing our minds artificially to the desire for knowledge. The existence of this desire for knowledge about the relation of man to the world proves that the naïve point of view must be abandoned. If the naïve point of view yielded anything which we could acknowledge as truth, we could not experience this desire. But mere abandonment of the naïve point of view does not lead to any other view which we could regard as true, so long as we retain, without noticing it, the type of theory which the naïve point of view imposes on us. This is the mistake made by the man who says, I experience only my ideas, and though I think that I am dealing with real things, I am actually conscious of nothing but my ideas of real things. I must, therefore, suppose that genuine realities, "things-in-themselves," exist only outside the boundary of my consciousness; that they are inaccessible to my immediate knowledge; but that they somehow come into contact with me and influence me so as to make a world of ideas arise in me. Whoever thinks thus, duplicates in thought the world before him by adding another. But, strictly he ought to begin his whole theorising over again with regard to this second world. For the unknown "thing-in-itself," in its relation to man's own nature, is conceived in exactly the same way as is the known thing of the naïvely realistic point of view. There is only one way of escaping from the confusion into which one falls, by critical reflection on this naïve point of view. This is to observe that, at the very heart of everything we can experience, be it within the mind or outside in the world of perception, there is something which does not share the fate of an idea interposing itself between the real event and the contemplating mind. This something is thinking. With regard to thinking we can maintain the point of view of Naïve Realism. If we mistakenly abandon it, it is only because we have learnt that we must abandon it for other mental activities, but overlook that what we have found to be true for other activities, does not apply to thinking. When we realise this, we gain access to the further insight that, in thinking and through thinking, man necessarily comes to know the very thing to which he appears to blind himself by interposing between the world and himself the stream of his ideas. A critic highly esteemed by the author of this book has objected that this discussion of thinking stops at a naïvely realistic theory of thinking, as shown by the fact that the real world and the world of ideas are held to be identical. However, the author believes himself to have shown in this very discussion that the validity of "Naïve Realism," as applied to thinking, results inevitably from an unprejudiced study of thinking; and that Naïve Realism, in so far as it is invalid for other mental activities, is overcome through the recognition of the true nature of thinking.

1

Knowledge is transcendental when it is aware that nothing can be asserted directly about the thing-in-itself but makes indirect inferences from the subjective which is known to the unknown which lies beyond the subjective (transcendental). The thing-in-itself is, according to this view, beyond the sphere of the world of immediate experience; in other words, it is transcendent. Our world can, however, be transcendentally related to the transcendent. Hartmann's theory is called Realism because it proceeds from the subjective, the mental, to the transcendent, the real.

VI

HUMAN INDIVIDUALITY

Philosophers have found the chief difficulty in the explanation of ideas in the fact that we are not identical with the external objects, and yet our ideas must have a form corresponding to their objects. But on closer inspection it turns out that this difficulty does not really exist. We certainly are not identical with the external things, but we belong together with them to one and the same world. The stream of the universal cosmic process passes through that segment of the world which, to my perception, is myself as subject. So far as my perception goes, I am, in the first instance, confined within the limits bounded by my skin. But all that is contained within the skin belongs to the cosmos as a whole. Hence, for a relation to subsist between my organism and an object external to me, it is by no means necessary that something of the object should slip into me, or make an impression on my mind, like a signet-ring on wax. The question, How do I gain knowledge of that tree ten feet away from me, is utterly misleading. It springs from the view that the boundaries of my body are absolute barriers, through which information about external things filters into me. The forces which are active within my body are the same as those which exist outside. I am, therefore, really identical with the objects; not, however, I in so far as I am subject of perception, but I in so far as I am a part within the universal cosmic process. The percept of the tree belongs to the same whole as my Self. The universal cosmic process produces alike, here the percept of the tree, and there the percept of my Self. Were I a world-creator instead of a world-knower, subject and object (percept and self) would originate in one act. For they condition one another reciprocally. As world-knower I can discover the common element in both, so far as they are complementary aspects of the world, only through thought which by means of concepts relates the one to the other.

The most difficult to drive from the field are the so-called physiological proofs of the subjectivity of our percepts. When I exert pressure on the skin of my body, I experience it as a pressure sensation. This same pressure can be sensed as light by the eye, as sound by the ear. I experience an electrical shock by the eye as light, by the ear as sound, by the nerves of the skin as touch, and by the nose as a smell of phosphorus. What follows from these facts? Only this: I experience an electrical shock, or, as the case may be, a pressure followed by a light, or a sound, or, it may be, a certain smell, etc. If there were no eye present, then no light quality would accompany the perception of the mechanical vibrations in my environment; without the presence of the ear, no sound, etc. But what right have we to say that in the absence of sense-organs the whole process would not exist at all? All those who, from the fact that an electrical process causes a sensation of light in the eye, conclude that what we sense as light is only a mechanical process of motion, forget that they are only arguing from one percept to another, and not at all to something altogether transcending percepts. Just as we can say that the eye perceives a mechanical process of motion in its surroundings as light, so we can affirm that every change in an object, determined by natural law, is perceived by us as a process of motion. If I draw twelve pictures of a horse on the circumference of a rotating disc, reproducing exactly the positions which the horse's body successively assumes in movement, I can, by rotating the disc, produce the illusion of movement. I need only look through an opening in such a way that, at regular intervals, I perceive the successive positions of the horse. I perceive, not separate pictures of twelve horses, but one picture of a single galloping horse.

The above-mentioned physiological facts cannot, therefore, throw any light on the relation of percept to idea. Hence, we must seek a relation some other way.

The moment a percept appears in my field of consciousness, thought, too, becomes active in me. A member of my thought-system, a definite intuition, a concept, connects itself with the percept. When, next, the percept disappears from my field of vision, what remains? The intuition, with the reference to the particular percept which it acquired in the moment of perception. The degree of vividness with which I can subsequently recall this reference depends on the manner in which my mental and bodily organism is working. An idea is nothing but an intuition related to a particular percept; it is a concept which was once connected with a certain percept, and which retains this reference to the percept. My concept of a lion is not constructed out of my percepts of a lion; but my idea of a lion is formed under the guidance of the percepts. I can teach someone to form the concept of a lion without his ever having seen a lion, but I can never give him a living idea of it without the help of his own perception.

An idea is therefore nothing but an individualised concept. And now we can see how real objects can be represented to us by ideas. The full reality of a thing is present to us in the moment of observation through the combination of concept and percept. The concept acquires by means of the percept an individualised form, a relation to this particular percept. In this individualised form which carries with it, as an essential feature, the reference to the percept, it continues to exist in us and constitutes the idea of the thing in question. If we come across a second thing with which the same concept connects itself, we recognise the second as being of the same kind as the first; if we come across the same thing twice, we find in our conceptual system, not merely a corresponding concept, but the individualised concept with its characteristic relation to this same object, and thus we recognise the object again.

The idea, then, stands between the percept and the concept. It is the determinate concept which points to the percept.

The sum of my ideas may be called my experience. The man who has the greater number of individualised concepts will be the man of richer experience. A man who lacks all power of intuition is not capable of acquiring experience. The objects simply disappear again from the field of his consciousness, because he lacks the concepts which he ought to bring into relation with them. On the other hand, a man whose faculty of thought is well developed, but whose perception functions badly owing to his clumsy sense-organs, will be no better able to gain experience. He can, it is true, by one means and another acquire concepts; but the living reference to particular objects is lacking to his intuitions. The unthinking traveller and the student absorbed in abstract conceptual systems are alike incapable of acquiring a rich experience.

Reality presents itself to us as the union of percept and concept; and the subjective representation of this reality presents itself to us as idea.

If our personality expressed itself only in cognition, the totality of all that is objective would be contained in percept, concept and idea.

However, we are not satisfied merely to refer percepts, by means of thinking, to concepts, but we relate them also to our private subjectivity, our individual Ego. The expression of this relation to us as individuals is feeling, which manifests itself as pleasure and pain.

Thinking and feeling correspond to the two-fold nature of our being to which reference has already been made. By means of thought we take an active part in the universal cosmic process. By means of feeling we withdraw ourselves into the narrow precincts of our own being.

Thought links us to the world; feeling leads us back into ourselves and thus makes us individuals. Were we merely thinking and perceiving beings, our whole life would flow along in monotonous indifference. Could we only know ourselves as Selves, we should be totally indifferent to ourselves. It is only because with self-knowledge we experience self-feeling, and with the perception of objects pleasure and pain, that we live as individuals whose existence is not exhausted by the conceptual relations in which they stand to the rest of the world, but who have a special value in themselves.

One might be tempted to regard the life of feeling as something more richly saturated with reality than the apprehension of the world by thought. But the reply to this is that the life of feeling, after all, has this richer meaning only for my individual self. For the universe as a whole my feelings can be of value only if, as percepts of myself, they enter into connection with a concept and in this roundabout way become links in the cosmos.

Our life is a continual oscillation between our share in the universal world-process and our own individual existence. The farther we ascend into the universal nature of thought where the individual, at last, interests us only as an example, an instance, of the concept, the more the character of something individual, of the quite determinate, unique personality, becomes lost in us. The farther we descend into the depths of our own private life and allow the vibrations of our feelings to accompany all our experiences of the outer world, the more we cut ourselves off from the universal life. True individuality belongs to him whose feelings reach up to the farthest possible extent into the region of the ideal. There are men in whom even the most general ideas still bear that peculiar personal tinge which shows unmistakably their connection with their author. There are others whose concepts come before us as devoid of any trace of individual colouring as if they had not been produced by a being of flesh and blood at all.

Even ideas give to our conceptual life an individual stamp. Each one of us has his special standpoint from which he looks out on the world. His concepts link themselves to his percepts. He has his own special way of forming general concepts. This special character results for each of us from his special standpoint in the world, from the way in which the range of his percepts is dependent on the place in the whole where he exists. The conditions of individuality here indicated, we call the milieu.

This special character of our experience must be distinguished from another which depends on our peculiar organisation. Each of us, as we know, is organised as a unique, fully determined individual. Each of us combines special feelings, and these in the most varying degrees of intensity, with his percepts. This is just the individual element in the personality of each of us. It is what remains over when we have allowed fully for all the determining factors in our milieu.

A life of feeling, wholly devoid of thought, would gradually lose all connection with the world. But man is meant to be a whole, and knowledge of objects will go hand-in-hand for him with the development and education of the feeling-side of his nature.

Feeling is the means whereby, in the first instance, concepts gain concrete life.

VII

ARE THERE ANY LIMITS TO KNOWLEDGE?

We have established that the elements for the explanation of reality are to be taken from the two spheres of perception and thought. It is due, as we have seen, to our organisation that the full totality of reality, including our own selves as subjects, appears at first as a duality. Knowledge transcends this duality by fusing the two elements of reality, the percept and the concept, into the complete thing. Let us call the manner in which the world presents itself to us, before by means of knowledge it has taken on its true nature, "the world of appearance," in distinction from the unified whole composed of percept and concept. We can then say, The world is given to us as a duality (Dualism), and knowledge transforms it into a unity (Monism). A philosophy which starts from this basal principle may be called a Monistic philosophy, or Monism. Opposed to this is the theory of two worlds, or Dualism. The latter does not, by any means, assume merely that there are two sides of a single reality, which are kept apart by our organisation, but that there are two worlds totally distinct from one another. It then tries to find in one of these two worlds the principle of explanation for the other.

Dualism rests on a false conception of what we call knowledge. It divides the whole of reality into two spheres, each of which has its own laws, and it leaves these two worlds standing outside one another.

It is from a Dualism such as this that there arises the distinction between the object of perception and the thing-in-itself, which Kant introduced into philosophy, and which, to the present day, we have not succeeded in expelling. According to our interpretation, it is due to the nature of our organisation that a particular object can be given to us only as a percept. Thought transcends this particularity by assigning to each percept its proper place in the world as a whole. As long as we determine the separate parts of the cosmos as percepts, we are simply following, in this sorting out, a law of our subjective constitution. If, however, we regard all percepts, taken together, merely as one part, and contrast with this a second part, viz., the things-in-themselves, then our philosophy is building castles-in-the-air. We are then engaged in mere playing with concepts. We construct an artificial opposition, but we can find no content for the second of these opposites, seeing that no content for a particular thing can be found except in perception.

Every kind of reality which is assumed to exist outside the sphere of perception and conception must be relegated to the limbo of unverified hypotheses. To this category belongs the "thing-in-itself." It is, of course, quite natural that a Dualistic thinker should be unable to find the connection between the world-principle which he hypothetically assumes and the facts that are given in experience. For the hypothetical world-principle itself a content can be found only by borrowing it from experience and shutting one's eyes to the fact of the borrowing. Otherwise it remains an empty and meaningless concept, a mere form without content. In this case the Dualistic thinker generally asserts that the content of this concept is inaccessible to our knowledge. We can know only that such a content exists, but not what it is. In either case it is impossible to transcend Dualism. Even though one were to import a few abstract elements from the world of experience into the content of the thing-in-itself, it would still remain impossible to reduce the rich concrete life of experience to those few elements, which are, after all, themselves taken from experience. Du Bois-Reymond lays it down that the imperceptible atoms of matter produce sensation and feeling by means of their position and motion, and then infers from this premise that we can never find a satisfactory explanation of how matter and motion produce sensation and feeling, for "it is absolutely and for ever unintelligible that it should be other than indifferent to a number of atoms of carbon, hydrogen, and nitrogen, etc., how they lie and move, how they lay or moved, or how they will lie and will move. It is in no way intelligible how consciousness can come into existence through their interaction." This conclusion is characteristic of the whole tendency of this school of thought. Position and motion are abstracted from the rich world of percepts. They are then transferred to the fictitious world of atoms. And then we are astonished that we fail to evolve concrete life out of this principle of our own making, which we have borrowed from the world of percepts.

That the Dualist, working as he does with a completely empty concept of the thing-in-itself, can reach no explanation of the world, follows from the very definition of his principle which has been given above.

In any case, the Dualist finds it necessary to set impassable barriers to our faculty of knowledge. A follower of the Monistic theory of the world knows that all he needs to explain any given phenomenon in the world is to be found within this world itself. What prevents him from finding it can be only chance limitations in space and time, or defects of his organisation, *i.e.*, not of human organisation in general, but only of his own.

It follows from the concept of knowledge, as defined by us, that there can be no talk of any limits of knowledge. Knowledge is not a concern of the universe in general, but one which men must settle for themselves. External things demand no explanation. They exist and act on one another according to laws which thought can discover. They exist in indivisible unity with these laws. But we, in our self-hood, confront them, grasping at first only what we have called percepts. However, within ourselves we find the power to discover also the other part of reality. Only when the Self has combined for itself the two elements of reality which are indivisibly bound up with one another in the world, is our thirst for knowledge stilled. The Self is then again in contact with reality.

The presuppositions for the development of knowledge thus exist through and for the Self. It is the Self which sets itself the problems of knowledge. It takes them from thought, an element which in itself is absolutely clear and transparent. If we set ourselves questions which we cannot answer, it must be because the content of the questions is not in all respects clear and distinct. It is not the world which sets questions to us, but we who set them to ourselves.

I can imagine that it would be quite impossible for me to answer a question which I happened to find written down somewhere, without knowing the universe of discourse from which the content of the question is taken.

In knowledge we are concerned with questions which arise for us through the fact that a world of percepts, conditioned by time, space, and our subjective organisation, stands over against a world of concepts expressing the totality of the universe. Our task consists in the assimilation to one another of these two spheres, with both of which we are familiar. There is no room here for talking about limits of knowledge. It may be that, at a particular moment, this or that remains unexplained because, through chance obstacles, we are prevented from perceiving the things involved. What is not found to-day, however, may easily be found to-morrow. The limits due to these causes are only contingent, and must be overcome by the progress of perception and thought.

Dualism makes the mistake of transferring the opposition of subject and object, which has meaning only within the perceptual world, to pure conceptual entities outside this world. Now the distinct and separate things in the perceptual world remain separated only so long as the perceiver refrains from thinking. For thought cancels all separation and reveals it as due to purely subjective conditions. The Dualist, therefore, transfers to entities transcending the perceptual world abstract determinations which, even in the perceptual world, have no absolute, but only relative, validity. He thus divides the two factors concerned in the process of knowledge, viz., percept and concept, into four: (1) the object in itself; (2) the percept which the subject has of the object; (3) the subject; (4) the concept which relates the percept to the object in itself. The relation between subject and object is "real"; the subject is really (dynamically) influenced by the object. This real process does not appear in consciousness. But it evokes in the subject a response to the stimulation from the object. The result of this response is the percept. This, at length, appears in consciousness. The object has an objective (independent of the subject) reality, the percept a subjective reality. This subjective reality is referred by the subject to the object. This reference is an ideal one. Dualism thus divides the process of knowledge into two parts. The one part, viz., the production of the perceptual object by the thing-in-itself, he conceives of as taking place outside consciousness, whereas the other, the combination of percept with concept and the latter's reference to the thing-in-itself, takes place, according to him, in consciousness.

With such presuppositions, it is clear why the Dualist regards his concepts merely as subjective representations of what is really external to his consciousness. The objectively real process in the subject by means of which the percept is produced, and still more the objective relations between things-in-themselves, remain for the Dualist inaccessible to direct knowledge. According to him, man can get only conceptual representations of the objectively real. The bond of unity which connects things-in-themselves with one another, and also objectively with the individual minds (as things-in-themselves) of each of us, exists beyond our consciousness in a Divine Being of whom, once more, we have merely a conceptual representation.

The Dualist believes that the whole world would be dissolved into a mere abstract scheme of concepts, did he not posit the existence of real connections beside the conceptual ones. In other words, the ideal principles which thinking discovers are too airy for the Dualist, and he seeks, in addition, real principles with which to support them.

Let us examine these real principles a little more closely. The naïve man (Naïve Realist) regards the objects of sense-experience as realities. The fact that his hands can grasp, and his eyes see, these objects is for him sufficient guarantee of their reality. "Nothing exists that cannot be perceived" is, in fact, the first axiom of the naïve man; and it is held to be equally valid in its converse: "Everything which is perceived exists." The best proof for this assertion is the naïve man's belief in immortality and in ghosts. He thinks of the soul as a fine kind of matter perceptible by the senses which, in special circumstances, may actually become visible to the ordinary man (belief in ghosts).

In contrast with this, his real, world, the Naïve Realist regards everything else, especially the world of ideas, as unreal, or "merely ideal." What we add to objects by thinking is merely thoughts about the objects. Thought adds nothing real to the percept.

But it is not only with reference to the existence of things that the naïve man regards perception as the sole guarantee of reality, but also with reference to the existence of processes. A thing, according to him, can act on another only when a force actually present to perception issues from the one and acts upon the other. The older physicists thought that very fine kinds of substances emanate from the objects and penetrate through the sense-organs into the soul. The actual perception of these substances is impossible only because of the coarseness of our sense-organs relatively to the fineness of these substances. In principle, the reason for attributing reality to these substances was the same as that for attributing it to the objects of the sensible world, viz., their kind of existence, which was conceived to be analogous to that of perceptual reality.

The self-contained being of ideas is not thought of by the naïve mind as real in the same sense. An object conceived "merely in idea" is regarded as a chimera until sense-perception can furnish proof of its reality. In short, the naïve man demands, in addition to the ideal evidence of his thinking, the real evidence of his senses. In this need of the naïve man lies the ground for the origin of the belief in revelation. The God whom we apprehend by thought remains always merely our idea of God. The naïve consciousness demands that God should manifest Himself in ways accessible to the senses. God must appear in the flesh, and must attest his Godhead to our senses by the changing of water into wine.

Even knowledge itself is conceived by the naïve mind as a process analogous to sense-perception. Things, it is thought, make an impression on the mind, or send out copies of themselves which enter through our senses, etc.

What the naïve man can perceive with his senses he regards as real, and what he cannot perceive (God, soul, knowledge, etc.) he regards as analogous to what he can perceive.

On the basis of Naïve Realism, science can consist only in an exact description of the content of perception. Concepts are only means to this end. They exist to provide ideal counterparts of percepts. With the things themselves they have nothing to do. For the Naïve Realist only the individual tulips, which we can see, are real. The universal idea of tulip is to him an abstraction, the unreal thought-picture which the mind constructs for itself out of the characteristics common to all tulips.

Naïve Realism, with its fundamental principle of the reality of all percepts, contradicts experience, which teaches us that the content of percepts is of a transitory nature. The tulip I see is real to-day; in a year it will have vanished into nothingness. What persists is the species "tulip." This species is, however, for the Naïve Realist merely an idea, not a reality. Thus this theory of the world finds itself in the paradoxical position of seeing its realities arise and perish, while that which, by contrast with its realities, it regards as unreal endures. Hence Naïve Realism is compelled to acknowledge the existence of something ideal by the side of percepts. It must include within itself entities which cannot be perceived by the senses. In admitting them, it escapes contradicting itself by conceiving their existence as analogous to that of objects of sense. Such hypothetical realities are the invisible forces by means of which the objects of sense-perception act on one another. Another such reality is heredity, the effects of which survive the individual, and which is the reason why from the individual a new being develops which is similar to it, and by means of which the species is maintained. The soul, the life-principle permeating the organic body, is another such reality which the naïve mind is always found conceiving in analogy to realities of sense-perception. And, lastly, the Divine Being, as conceived by the naïve mind, is such a hypothetical entity. The Deity is thought of as acting in a manner exactly corresponding to that which we can perceive in man himself, *i.e.*, the Deity is conceived anthropomorphically.

Modern Physics traces sensations back to the movements of the smallest particles of bodies and of an infinitely fine substance, called ether. What we experience, *e.g.*, as warmth is a movement of the parts of a body which causes the warmth in the space occupied by that body. Here again something imperceptible is conceived on the analogy of what is perceptible. Thus, in terms of perception, the analogon to the concept "body" is, say, the interior of a room, shut in on all sides, in which elastic balls are moving in all directions, impinging one on another, bouncing on and off the walls, etc.

Without such assumptions the world of the Naïve Realist would collapse into a disconnected chaos of percepts, without mutual relations, and having no unity within itself. It is clear, however, that Naïve Realism can make these assumptions only by contradicting itself. If it would remain true to its fundamental principle, that only what is perceived is real, then it ought not to assume a reality where it perceives nothing. The imperceptible forces of which perceptible things are the bearers are, in fact, illegitimate hypotheses from the standpoint of Naïve Realism. But because Naïve Realism knows no other realities, it invests its hypothetical forces with perceptual content. It thus transfers a form of existence (the existence of percepts) to a sphere where the only means of making any assertion concerning such existence, viz., sense-perception, is lacking.

This self-contradictory theory leads to Metaphysical Realism. The latter constructs, beside the perceptible reality, an imperceptible one which it conceives on the analogy of the former. Metaphysical Realism is, therefore, of necessity Dualistic.

Wherever the Metaphysical Realist observes a relation between perceptible things (mutual approach through movement, the entrance of an object into consciousness, etc.), there he posits a reality. However, the relation of which he becomes aware cannot be perceived but only expressed by means of thought. The ideal relation is thereupon arbitrarily assimilated to something perceptible. Thus, according to this theory, the world is composed of the objects of perception which are in ceaseless flux, arising and disappearing, and of imperceptible forces by which the perceptible objects are produced, and which are permanent.

Metaphysical Realism is a self-contradictory mixture of Naïve Realism and Idealism. Its forces are imperceptible entities endowed with the qualities proper to percepts. The Metaphysical Realist has made up his mind to acknowledge in addition to the sphere for the existence of which he has an instrument of knowledge in sense-perception, the existence of another sphere for which this instrument fails, and which can be known only by means of thought. But he cannot make up his mind at the same time to acknowledge that the mode of existence which thought reveals, viz., the concept (or idea), has equal rights with percepts. If we are to avoid the contradiction of imperceptible percepts, we must admit that, for us, the relations which thought traces between percepts can have no other mode of existence than that of concepts. If one rejects the untenable part of Metaphysical Realism, there remains the concept of the world as the aggregate of percepts and their conceptual (ideal) relations. Metaphysical Realism, then, merges itself in a view of the world according to which the principle of perceptibility holds for percepts, and that of conceivability for the relations between the percepts. This view of the world has no room, in addition to the perceptual and conceptual worlds, for a third sphere in which both principles, the so-called "real" principle and the "ideal" principle, are simultaneously valid.

When the Metaphysical Realist asserts that, beside the ideal relation between the perceived object and the perceiving subject, there must be a real relation between the percept as "thing-in-itself" and the subject as "thing-in-itself" (the so-called individual mind), he is basing his assertion on the false assumption of a real process, imperceptible but analogous to the processes in the world of percepts. Further, when the Metaphysical Realist asserts that we stand in a conscious ideal relation to our world of percepts, but that to the real world we can have only a dynamic (force) relation, he repeats the mistake we have already criticised. We can talk of a dynamic relation only within the world of percepts (in the sphere of the sense of touch), but not outside that world.

Let us call the view which we have just characterised, and into which Metaphysical Realism merges when it discards its contradictory elements, Monism, because it combines one-sided Realism and Idealism into a higher unity.

For Naïve Realism, the real world is an aggregate of percepts; for Metaphysical Realism, reality belongs not only to percepts but also to imperceptible forces; Monism replaces forces by ideal relations which are supplied by thought. These relations are the laws of nature. A law of nature is nothing but the conceptual expression for the connection of certain percepts.

Monism is never called upon to ask whether there are any principles of explanation for reality other than percepts and concepts. The Monist knows that in the whole realm of the real there is no occasion for this question. In the perceptual world, as immediately apprehended, he sees one-half of reality; in the union of this world with the world of concepts he finds full reality. The Metaphysical Realist might object that, relatively to our organisation, our knowledge may be complete in itself, that no part may be lacking, but that we do not know how the world appears to a mind organised differently from our own. To this the Monist will reply, Maybe there are intelligences other than human; and maybe also that their percepts are different from ours, if they have perception at all. But this is irrelevant to me for the following reasons. Through my perceptions, *i.e.*, through this specifically human mode of perception, I, as subject, am confronted with the object. The nexus of things is thereby broken. The subject reconstructs the nexus by means of thought. In doing so it re-inserts itself into the context of the world as a whole. As it is only through the Self, as subject, that the whole appears rent in two between percept and concept, the reunion of those two factors will give us complete knowledge. For beings with a different perceptual world (*e.g.*, if they had twice our number of sense-organs) the nexus would appear broken in another place, and the reconstruction would accordingly have to take a form specifically adapted to such beings. The question concerning the limits of knowledge troubles only Naïve and Metaphysical Realism, both of which see in the contents of mind only ideal representations of the real world. For, to these theories, whatever falls outside the subject is something absolute, a self-contained whole, and the subject's mental content is a copy which is wholly external to this absolute. The completeness of knowledge depends on the greater or lesser degree of resemblance between the representation and the absolute object. A being with fewer senses than man will perceive less of the world, one with more senses will perceive more. The former's knowledge will, therefore, be less complete than the latter's.

For Monism, the situation is different. The point where the unity of the world appears to be rent asunder into subject and object depends on the organisation of the percipient. The object is not absolute but merely relative to the nature of the subject. The bridging of the gap, therefore, can take place only in the quite specific way which is characteristic of the human subject. As soon as the Self, which in perception is set over against the world, is again re-inserted into the world-nexus by constructive thought, all further questioning ceases, having been but a result of the separation.

A differently constituted being would have a differently constituted knowledge. Our own knowledge suffices to answer the questions which result from our own mental constitution.

Metaphysical Realism must ask, What is it that gives us our percepts? What is it that stimulates the subject?

Monism holds that percepts are determined by the subject. But in thought the subject has, at the same time, the instrument for transcending this determination of which it is itself the author.

The Metaphysical Realist is faced by a further difficulty when he seeks to explain the similarity of the world-views of different human individuals. He has to ask himself, How is it that my theory of the world, built up out of subjectively determined percepts and out of concepts, turns out to be the same as that which another individual is also building up out of these same two subjective factors? How, in any case, is it possible for me to argue from my own subjective view of the world to that of another human being? The Metaphysical Realist thinks he can infer the similarity of the subjective world-views of different human beings from their ability to get on with one another in practical life. From this similarity of world-views he infers further the likeness to one another of individual minds, meaning by "individual mind" the "I-in-itself" underlying each subject.

We have here an inference from a number of effects to the character of the underlying causes. We believe that after we have observed a sufficiently large number of instances, we know the connection sufficiently to know how the inferred causes will act in other instances. Such an inference is called an inductive inference. We shall be obliged to modify its results, if further observation yields some unexpected fact, because the character of our conclusion is, after all, determined only by the particular details of our actual observations. The Metaphysical Realist asserts that this knowledge of causes, though restricted by these conditions, is quite sufficient for practical life.

Inductive inference is the fundamental method of modern Metaphysical Realism. At one time it was thought that out of concepts we could evolve something that would no longer be a concept. It was thought that the metaphysical reals, which Metaphysical Realism after all requires, could be known by means of concepts. This method of philosophising is now out of date. Instead it is thought that from a sufficiently large number of perceptual facts we can infer the character of the thing-in-itself which lies behind these facts. Formerly it was from concepts, now it is from percepts, that the Realist seeks to evolve the metaphysically real. Because concepts are before the mind in transparent clearness, it was thought that we might deduce from them the metaphysically real with absolute certainty. Percepts are not given with the same transparent clearness. Each fresh one is a little different from others of the same kind which preceded it. In principle, therefore, anything inferred from past experience is somewhat modified by each subsequent experience. The character of the metaphysically real thus obtained can therefore be only relatively true, for it is open to correction by further instances. The character of Von Hartmann's Metaphysics depends on this methodological principle. The motto on the title-page of his first important book is, "Speculative results gained by the inductive method of Science."

The form which the Metaphysical Realist at the present day gives to his things-in-themselves is obtained by inductive inferences. Consideration of the process of knowledge has convinced him of the existence of an objectively-real world-nexus, over and above the subjective world which we know by means of percepts and concepts. The nature of this reality he thinks he can determine by inductive inferences from his percepts.

Addition to the Revised Edition (1918).

The unprejudiced study of experience, in perceiving and conceiving, such as we have attempted to describe it in the preceding chapters, is liable to be interfered with again and again by certain ideas which spring from the soil of natural science. Thus, taking our stand on science, we say that the eye perceives in the spectrum colours from red to violet. But beyond violet there lie rays within the compass of the spectrum to which corresponds, not a colour perceived by the eye, but a chemical effect. Similarly, beyond the rays which make us perceive red, there are rays which have only heat effects. These and similar phenomena lead, on reflection, to the view that the range of man's perceptual world is defined by the range of his senses, and that he would perceive a very different world if he had additional, or altogether different, senses. Those who like to indulge in far-roaming fancies in this direction, for which the brilliant discoveries of recent scientific research provide a highly tempting occasion, may well be led to confess that nothing enters the field of man's observation except what can affect his senses, as these have been determined by his whole organisation. Man has no right to regard his percepts, limited as these are by his organisation, as in any way a standard to which reality must conform. Every new sense would confront him with a different picture of reality. Within its proper limits, this is a wholly justified view. But if anyone lets himself be confused by this view in the unprejudiced study of the relation of percept and concept, as set forth in these chapters, he blocks the path for himself to a knowledge of man and the world which is rooted in reality. The experience of the essential nature of thought, *i.e.*, the active construction of the world of concepts, is something wholly different from the experience of a perceptible object through the senses. Whatever additional senses man might have, not one would give him reality, if his thinking did not organise with its concepts whatever he perceived by means of such a sense. Every sense, whatever its kind, provided only it is organised by thought, enables man to live right in the real. The fancy-picture of other perceptual worlds, made possible by other senses, has nothing to do with the problem of how it is that man stands in the midst of reality. We must clearly understand that every perceptual picture of the world owes its form to the physical organisation of the percipient, but that only the percepts which have been organised by the living labour of thought lead us into reality. Fanciful speculations concerning the way the world would appear to other than human souls, can give us no occasion to want to understand man's relation to the world. Such a desire comes only with the recognition that every percept presents only a part of the reality it contains, and that, consequently, it leads us away from its own proper reality. This recognition is supplemented by the further one that thinking leads us into the part of reality which the percept conceals in itself. Another difficulty in the way of the unprejudiced study of the relation we have here described, between percept and concept as elaborated by thought, may be met with occasionally, when in the field of physics the necessity arises of speaking, not of immediately perceptible elements, but of non-perceptible magnitudes, such as, *e.g.*, lines of electric or magnetic force. It may seem as if the elements of reality of which physicists speak, had no connection either with what is perceptible, or with the concepts which active thinking has elaborated. Yet such a view would depend on self-deception. The main point is that all the results of physical research, except illegitimate hypotheses which ought to be excluded, have been gained through perceiving and conceiving. Entities which are seemingly non-perceptible, are referred by the physicists' sound instinct for knowledge to the field in which actual percepts lie, and they are dealt with in thought by means of the concepts which are commonly applied in this field. The magnitudes in a field of electric or magnetic force are reached, in their essence, by no other cognitive process than the one which connects percept and concept.—An increase or a modification of human senses would yield a different perceptual picture, an enrichment or a modification of human experience. But genuine knowledge could be gained out of this new experience only through the mutual co-operation of concept and percept. The deepening of knowledge depends on the powers of intuition which express themselves in thinking (see page 90). Intuition may, in those experiences in which thinking expresses itself, dive either into deeper or shallower levels of reality. An expansion of the perceptual picture may supply stimuli for, and thus indirectly promote, this diving of intuition. But this diving into the depth, through which we attain reality, ought never to be confused with the contrast between a wider and a narrower perceptual picture, which always contains only half of reality, as that is conditioned by the structure of the knower's organism. Those who do not lose themselves in abstractions will understand how for a knowledge of human nature the fact is relevant, that physics must infer the existence, in the field of percepts, of elements to which no sense is adapted as it is to colour or sound. Human nature, taken concretely, is determined not only by what, in virtue of his physical organisation, man opposes to himself as immediate percept, but also by all else which he excludes from this immediate percept. Just as life needs unconscious sleep alongside of conscious waking experience, so man's experience of himself needs over and above the sphere of his sense-perception another sphere—and a much bigger one—of non-perceptible elements belonging to the same field from which the percepts of the senses come. Implicitly all this was already laid down in the original argument of this book. The author adds the present amplification of the argument, because he has found by experience that some readers have not read attentively enough. It is to be remembered, too, that the idea of perception, developed in this book, is not to be confused with the idea of external sense-perception which is but a special case of the former. The reader will gather from what has preceded, but even more from what will be expounded later, that everything is here taken as "percept" which sensuously or spiritually enters into man's experience, so long as it has not yet been seized upon by the actively constructed concept. No "senses," as we ordinarily understand the term, are necessary in order to have percepts of a psychical or spiritual kind. It may be urged that this extension of ordinary usage is illegitimate. But the extension is absolutely indispensable, unless we are to be prevented by the current sense of a word from enlarging our knowledge of certain realms of facts. If we use "percept" only as meaning "sense-percept," we shall never advance beyond sense-percepts to a concept fit for the purposes of knowledge. It is sometimes necessary to enlarge a concept in order that it may get its appropriate meaning within a narrower field. Again, it is at times necessary to add to the original content of a concept, in order that the original thought may be justified or, perhaps, readjusted. Thus we find it said here in this book: "An idea is nothing but an individualised concept." It has been objected that this is a solecism. But this terminology is necessary if we are to find out what an idea really is. How can we expect any progress in knowledge, if every one who finds himself compelled to readjust concepts, is to be met by the objection: "This is a solecism"?

THE REALITY OF FREEDOM

VIII

THE FACTORS OF LIFE

Let us recapitulate the results gained in the previous chapters. The world appears to man as a multiplicity, as an aggregate of separate entities. He himself is one of these entities, a thing among things. Of this structure of the world we say simply that it is given, and inasmuch as we do not construct it by conscious activity, but simply find it, we say that it consists of percepts. Within this world of percepts we perceive ourselves. This percept of Self would remain merely one among many other percepts, did it not give rise to something which proves capable of connecting all percepts one with another and, therefore, the aggregate of all other percepts with the percept of Self. This something which emerges is no longer a mere percept; neither is it, like percepts, simply given. It is produced by our activity. It appears, in the first instance, bound up with what each of us perceives as his Self. In its inner significance, however, it transcends the Self. It adds to the separate percepts ideal determinations, which, however, are related to one another, and which are grounded in a whole. What self-perception yields is ideally determined by this something in the same way as all other percepts, and placed as subject, or "I," over against the objects. This something is thought, and the ideal determinations are the concepts and ideas. Thought, therefore, first manifests itself in connection with the percept of self. But it is not merely subjective, for the Self characterises itself as subject only with the help of thought. This relation of the Self to itself by means of thought is one of the fundamental determinations of our personal lives. Through it we lead a purely ideal existence. By means of it we are aware of ourselves as thinking beings. This determination of our lives would remain a purely conceptual (logical) one, if it were not supplemented by other determinations of our Selves. Our lives would then exhaust themselves in establishing ideal connections between percepts themselves, and between them and ourselves. If we call this establishment of an ideal relation an "act of cognition," and the resulting condition of ourselves "knowledge," then, assuming the above supposition to be true, we should have to consider ourselves as beings who merely apprehend or know.

The supposition is, however, untrue. We relate percepts to ourselves not merely ideally, through concepts, but also, as we have already seen, through feeling. In short, the content of our lives is not merely conceptual. The Naïve Realist holds that the personality actually lives more genuinely in the life of feeling than in the purely ideal activity of knowledge. From his point of view he is quite right in interpreting the matter in this way. Feeling plays on the subjective side exactly the part which percepts play on the objective side. From the principle of Naïve Realism, that everything is real which can be perceived, it follows that feeling is the guarantee of the reality of one's own personality. Monism, however, must bestow on feeling the same supplementation which it considers necessary for percepts, if these are to stand to us for reality in its full nature. For Monism, feeling is an incomplete reality, which, in the form in which it first appears to us, lacks as yet its second factor, the concept or idea. This is why, in actual life, feelings, like percepts, appear prior to knowledge. At first, we have merely a feeling of existence; and it is only in the course of our gradual development, that we attain to the point at which the concept of Self emerges from within the blind mass of feelings which fills our existence. However, what for us does not appear until later, is from the first indissolubly bound up with our feelings. This is how the naïve man comes to believe that in feeling he grasps existence immediately, in knowledge only mediately. The development of the affective life, therefore, appears to him more important than anything else. Not until he has grasped the unity of the world through feeling will he believe that he has comprehended it. He attempts to make feeling rather than thought the instrument of knowledge. Now a feeling is entirely individual, something equivalent to a percept. Hence a philosophy of feeling makes a cosmic principle out of something which has significance only within my own personality. Anyone who holds this view attempts to infuse his own self into the whole world. What the Monist strives to grasp by means of concepts the philosopher of feeling tries to attain through feeling, and he looks on his own felt union with objects as more immediate than knowledge.

The tendency just described, the philosophy of feeling, is Mysticism. The error in this view is that it seeks to possess by immediate experience what must be known, that it seeks to develop feeling, which is individual, into a universal principle.

A feeling is a purely individual activity. It is the relation of the external world to the subject, in so far as this relation finds expression in a purely subjective experience.

There is yet another expression of human personality. The Self, through thought, takes part in the universal world-life. Through thought it establishes purely ideal (conceptual) relations between percepts and itself, and between itself and percepts. In feeling, it has immediate experience of the relation of objects to itself as subject. In will, the opposite is the case. In volition, we are concerned once more with a percept, viz., that of the individual relation of the self to what is objective. Whatever in the act of will is not an ideal factor, is just as much mere object of perception as is any object in the external world.

Nevertheless, the Naïve Realist believes here again that he has before him something far more real than can ever be attained by thought. He sees in the will an element in which he is immediately aware of an activity, a causation, in contrast with thought which afterwards grasps this activity in conceptual form. On this view, the realisation by the Self of its will is a process which is experienced immediately. The adherent of this philosophy believes that in the will he has really got hold of one end of reality. Whereas he can follow other occurrences only from the outside by means of perception, he is confident that in his will he experiences a real process quite immediately. The mode of existence presented to him by the will within himself becomes for him the fundamental reality of the universe. His own will appears to him as a special case of the general world-process; hence the latter is conceived as a universal will. The will becomes the principle of reality just as, in Mysticism, feeling becomes the principle of knowledge. This kind of theory is called Voluntarism (Thelism). It makes something which can be experienced only individually the dominant factor of the world.

Voluntarism can as little be called scientific as can Mysticism. For both assert that the conceptual interpretation of the world is inadequate. Both demand, in addition to a principle of being which is ideal, also a principle which is real. But as perception is our only means of apprehending these so-called real principles, the assertion of Mysticism and Voluntarism coincides with the view that we have two sources of knowledge, viz., thought and perception, the latter finding individual expression as will and feeling. Since the immediate experiences which flow from the one source cannot be directly absorbed into the thoughts which flow from the other, perception (immediate experience) and thought remain side by side, without any higher form of experience to mediate between them. Beside the conceptual principle to which we attain by means of knowledge, there is also a real principle which must be immediately experienced. In other words, Mysticism and Voluntarism are both forms of Naïve Realism, because they subscribe to the doctrine that the immediately perceived (experienced) is real. Compared with Naïve Realism in its primitive form, they are guilty of the yet further inconsistency of accepting one definite form of perception (feeling, respectively will) as the exclusive means of knowing reality. Yet they can do this only so long as they cling to the general principle that everything that is perceived is real. They ought, therefore, to attach an equal value to external perception for purposes of knowledge.

Voluntarism turns into Metaphysical Realism, when it asserts the existence of will also in those spheres of reality in which will can no longer, as in the individual subject, be immediately experienced. It assumes hypothetically that a principle holds outside subjective experience, for the existence of which, nevertheless, subjective experience is the sole criterion. As a form of Metaphysical Realism, Voluntarism is open to the criticism developed in the preceding chapter, a criticism which makes it necessary to overcome the contradictory element in every form of Metaphysical Realism, and to recognise that the will is a universal world-process only in so far as it is ideally related to the rest of the world.

Addition to the Revised Edition (1918).

The difficulty of seizing the essential nature of thinking by observation lies in this, that it has generally eluded the introspecting mind all too easily by the time that the mind tries to bring it into the focus of attention. Nothing but the lifeless abstract, the corpse of living thought, then remains for inspection. When we consider only this abstract, we find it hard, by contrast, to resist yielding to the mysticism of feeling, or, again, to the metaphysics of will, both of which are "full of life." We are tempted to regard it as odd that anyone should want to seize the essence of reality in "mere thoughts." But if we once succeed in really holding fast the living essence of thinking, we learn to understand that the self-abandonment to feelings, or the intuiting of the will, cannot even be compared with the inward wealth of this life of thinking, which we experience as within itself ever at rest, yet at the same time ever in movement. Still less is it possible to rank will and feeling above thinking. It is owing precisely to this wealth, to this inward abundance of experience, that the image of thinking which presents itself to our ordinary attitude of mind, should appear lifeless and abstract. No other activity of the human mind is so easily misapprehended as thinking. Will and feeling still fill the mind with warmth even when we live through them again in memory. Thinking all too readily leaves us cold in recollection; it is as if the life of the mind had dried out. But this is really nothing but the strongly marked shadow thrown by its luminous, warm nature penetrating deeply into the phenomena of the world. This penetration is effected by the activity of thinking with a spontaneous outpouring of power—a power of spiritual love. There is no room here for the objection that thus to perceive love in the activity of thinking is to endow thinking with a feeling and a love which are not part of it. This objection is, in truth, a confirmation of the view here advocated. If we turn towards the essential nature of thinking, we find in it both feeling and will, and both these in their most profoundly real forms. If we turn away from thinking and towards "mere" feeling and will, these lose for us their genuine reality. If we are willing to make of thinking an intuitive experience, we can do justice, also, to experiences of the type of feeling and will. But the mysticism of feeling and the metaphysics of will do not know how to do justice to the penetration of reality which partakes at once of intuition and of thought. They conclude but too readily that they themselves are rooted in reality, but that the intuitive thinker, untouched by feeling, blind to reality, forms out of "abstract thoughts" a shadowy, chilly picture of the world.

IX

THE IDEA OF FREEDOM

The concept "tree" is conditioned for our knowledge by the percept "tree." There is only one determinate concept which I can select from the general system of concepts and apply to a given percept. The connection of concept and percept is mediately and objectively determined by thought in conformity with the percept. The connection between a percept and its concept is recognised after the act of perception, but the relevance of the one to the other is determined by the character of each.

Very different is the result when we consider knowledge, and, more particularly, the relation of man to the world which occurs in knowledge. In the preceding chapters the attempt has been made to show that an unprejudiced examination of this relation is able to throw light on its nature. A correct understanding of this examination leads to the conclusion that thinking may be intuitively apprehended in its unique, self-contained nature. Those who find it necessary, for the explanation of thinking as such, to invoke something else, *e.g.*, physical brain-processes, or unconscious spiritual processes lying behind the conscious thinking which they observe, fail to grasp the facts which an unprejudiced examination yields. When we observe our thinking, we live during the observation immediately within the essence of a spiritual, self-sustaining activity. Indeed, we may even affirm that if we want to grasp the essential nature of Spirit in the form in which it immediately presents itself to man, we need but look at our own self-sustaining thinking.

For the study of thinking two things coincide which elsewhere must always appear apart, viz., concept and percept. If we fail to see this, we shall be unable to regard the concepts which we have elaborated in response to percepts as anything but shadowy copies of these percepts, and we shall take the percepts as presenting to us reality as it really is. We shall, further, build up for ourselves a metaphysical world after the pattern of the world of percepts. We shall, each according to his habitual ideas, call this world a world of atoms, or of will, or of unconscious spirit, and so on. And we shall fail to notice that all the time we have been doing nothing but erecting hypothetically a metaphysical world modeled on the world we perceive. But if we clearly apprehend what thinking consists in, we shall recognise that percepts present to us only a portion of reality, and that the complementary portion which alone imparts to reality its full character as real, is experienced by us in the organisation of percepts by thought. We shall regard all thought, not as a shadowy copy of reality, but as a self-sustaining spiritual essence. We shall be able to say of it, that it is revealed to us in consciousness through intuition. Intuition is the purely spiritual conscious experience of a purely spiritual content. It is only through intuition that we can grasp the essence of thinking.

To win through, by means of unprejudiced observation, to the recognition of this truth of the intuitive essence of thinking requires an effort. But without this effort we shall not succeed in clearing the way for a theory of the psycho-physical organisation of man. We recognise that this organisation can produce no effect whatever on the essential nature of thinking. At first sight this seems to be contradicted by patent and obvious facts. For ordinary experience, human thinking occurs only in connection with, and by means of, such an organisation. This dependence on psycho-physical organisation is so prominent that its true bearing can be appreciated by us only if we recognise, that in the essential nature of thinking this organisation plays no part whatever. Once we appreciate this, we can no longer fail to notice how peculiar is the relation of human organisation to thought. For this organisation contributes nothing to the essential nature of thought, but recedes whenever thought becomes active. It suspends its own activity, it yields ground. And the ground thus set free is occupied by thought. The essence which is active in thought has a two-fold function: first it restricts the human organisation in its own activity; next, it steps into the place of that organisation. Yes, even the former, the restriction of human organisation, is an effect of the activity of thought, and more particularly of that part of it which prepares the manifestation of thinking. This explains the sense in which thinking has its counterpart in the organisation of the body. Once we perceive this, we can no longer misapprehend the significance for thinking of this physical counterpart.

When we walk over soft ground our feet leave deep tracks in the soil. We shall not be tempted to say that the forces of the ground, from below, have formed these tracks. We shall not attribute to these forces any share in the production of the tracks. Just so, if with open minds we observe the essential nature of thinking, we shall not attribute any share in that nature to the traces in the physical organism which thinking produces in preparing its manifestation through the body.[1]

An important question, however, confronts us here. If human organisation has no part in the essential nature of thinking, what is its function within the whole nature of man? Well, the effects of thinking upon this organisation have no bearing upon the essence of thinking, but they have a bearing upon the origin of the "I," or Ego-consciousness, through thinking. Thinking, in its unique character, constitutes the real Ego, but it does not constitute, as such, the Ego-consciousness. To see this we have but to study thinking with an open mind. The Ego is to be found in thinking. The Ego-consciousness arises through the traces which, in the sense above explained, the activity of thinking impresses upon our general consciousness. The Ego-consciousness thus arises through the physical organisation. This view must not, however, be taken to imply that the Ego-consciousness, once it has arisen, remains dependent on the physical organisation. On the contrary, once it exists it is taken up into thought and shares henceforth thought's spiritual self-subsistence.

The Ego-consciousness is built upon human organisation. The latter is the source of all acts of will. Following out the direction of the preceding exposition, we can gain insight into the connection of thought, conscious Ego, and act of will, only by studying first how an act of will issues from human organisation.[2]

In a particular act of will we must distinguish two factors: the motive and the spring of action. The motive is a factor of the nature of concept or idea; the spring of action is the factor in will which is directly determined in the human organisation. The conceptual factor, or motive, is the momentary determining cause of an act of will; the spring of action is the permanent determining factor in the individual. The motive of an act of will can be only a pure concept, or else a concept with a definite relation to perception, *i.e.*, an idea. Universal and individual concepts (ideas) become motives of will by influencing the human individual and determining him to action in a particular direction. One and the same concept, however, or one and the same idea, influence different individuals differently. They determine different men to different actions. An act of will is, therefore, not merely the outcome of a concept or an idea, but also of the individual make-up of human beings. This individual make-up we will call, following Eduard von Hartmann, the "characterological disposition." The manner in which concept and idea act on the characterological disposition of a man gives to his life a definite moral or ethical stamp.

The characterological disposition consists of the more or less permanent content of the individual's life, that is, of his habitual ideas and feelings. Whether an idea which enters my mind at this moment stimulates me to an act of will or not, depends on its relation to my other ideal contents, and also to my peculiar modes of feeling. My ideal content, in turn, is conditioned by the sum total of those concepts which have, in the course of my individual life, come in contact with percepts, that is, have become ideas. This, again, depends on my greater or lesser capacity for intuition, and on the range of my perception, that is, on the subjective and objective factors of my experiences, on the structure of my mind and on my environment. My affective life more especially determines my characterological disposition. Whether I shall make a certain idea or concept the motive for action will depend on whether it gives me pleasure or pain.

These are the factors which we have to consider in an act of will. The immediately present idea or concept, which becomes the motive, determines the end or the purpose of my will; my characterological disposition determines me to direct my activity towards this end. The idea of taking a walk in the next half-hour determines the end of my action. But this idea is raised to the level of a motive only if it meets with a suitable characterological disposition, that is, if during my past life I have formed the ideas of the wholesomeness of walking and the value of health; and, further, if the idea of walking is accompanied by a feeling of pleasure.

We must, therefore, distinguish (1) the possible subjective dispositions which are likely to turn given ideas and concepts into motives, and (2) the possible ideas and concepts which are capable of so influencing my characterological disposition that an act of will results. The former are for morality the springs of action, the latter its ends.

The springs of action in the moral life can be discovered by analysing the elements of which individual life is composed.

The first level of individual life is that of perception, more particularly sense-perception. This is the stage of our individual lives in which a percept translates itself into will immediately, without the intervention of either a feeling or a concept. The spring of action here involved may be called simply instinct. Our lower, purely animal, needs (hunger, sexual intercourse, etc.) find their satisfaction in this way. The main characteristic of instinctive life is the immediacy with which the percept starts off the act of will. This kind of determination of the will, which belongs originally only to the life of the lower senses, may, however, become extended also to the percepts of the higher senses. We may react to the percept of a certain event in the external world without reflecting on what we do, and without any special feeling connecting itself with the percept. We have examples of this especially in our ordinary conventional intercourse with men. The spring of this kind of action is called tact or moral good taste. The more often such immediate reactions to a percept occur, the more the agent will prove himself able to act purely under the guidance of tact; that is, tact becomes his characterological disposition.

The second level of human life is feeling. Definite feelings accompany the percepts of the external world. These feelings may become springs of action. When I see a hungry man, my pity for him may become the spring of my action. Such feelings, for example, are modesty, pride, sense of honour, humility, remorse, pity, revenge, gratitude, piety, loyalty, love, and duty.[3]

The third and last level of life is to have thoughts and ideas. An idea or a concept may become the motive of an action through mere reflection. Ideas become motives because, in the course of my life, I regularly connect certain aims of my will with percepts which recur again and again in a more or less modified form. Hence it is that, with men who are not wholly without experience, the occurrence of certain percepts is always accompanied also by the consciousness of ideas of actions, which they have themselves carried out in similar cases or which they have seen others carry out. These ideas float before their minds as determining models in all subsequent decisions; they become parts of their characterological disposition. We may give the name of practical experience to the spring of action just described. Practical experience merges gradually into purely tactful behaviour. That happens, when definite typical pictures of actions have become so closely connected in our minds with ideas of certain situations in life, that, in any given instance, we omit all deliberation based on experience and pass immediately from the percept to the action.

The highest level of individual life is that of conceptual thought without reference to any definite perceptual content. We determine the content of a concept through pure intuition on the basis of an ideal system. Such a concept contains, at first, no reference to any definite percepts. When an act of will comes about under the influence of a concept which refers to a percept, *i.e.*, under the influence of an idea, then it is the percept which determines our action indirectly by way of the concept. But when we act under the influence of pure intuitions, the spring of our action is pure thought. As it is the custom in philosophy to call pure thought "reason," we may perhaps be justified in giving the name of practical reason to the spring of action characteristic of this level of life. The clearest account of this spring of action has been given by Kreyenbühl (*Philosophische Monatshefte*, vol. xviii, No. 3). In my opinion his article on this subject is one of the most important contributions to present-day philosophy, more especially to Ethics. Kreyenbühl calls the spring of action, of which we are treating, the practical *a priori i.e.*, a spring of action issuing immediately from my intuition.

It is clear that such a spring of action can no longer be counted in the strictest sense as part of the characterological disposition. For what is here effective in me as a spring of action is no longer something purely individual, but the ideal, and hence universal, content of my intuition. As soon as I regard this content as the valid basis and starting-point of an action, I pass over into willing, irrespective of whether the concept was already in my mind beforehand, or whether it only occurs to me immediately before the action, that is, irrespective of whether it was present in the form of a disposition in me or not.

A real act of will results only when a present impulse to action, in the form of a concept or idea, acts on the characterological disposition. Such an impulse thereupon becomes the motive of the will.

The motives of moral conduct are ideas and concepts. There are Moralists who see in feeling also a motive of morality; they assert, *e.g.*, that the end of moral conduct is to secure the greatest possible quantity of pleasure for the agent. Pleasure itself, however, can never be a motive; at best only the idea of pleasure can act as motive. The idea of a future pleasure, but not the feeling itself, can act on my characterological disposition. For the feeling does not yet exist in the moment of action; on the contrary, it has first to be produced by the action.

The idea of one's own or another's well-being is, however, rightly regarded as a motive of the will. The principle of producing the greatest quantity of pleasure for oneself through one's action, that is, to attain individual happiness, is called Egoism. The attainment of this individual happiness is sought either by thinking ruthlessly only of one's own good, and striving to attain it even at the cost of the happiness of other individuals (Pure Egoism), or by promoting the good of others, either because one anticipates indirectly a favourable influence on one's own happiness through the happiness of others, or because one fears to endanger one's own interest by injuring others (Morality of Prudence). The special content of the egoistical principle of morality will depend on the ideas which we form of what constitutes our own, or others', good. A man will determine the content of his egoistical striving in accordance with what he regards as one of life's good things (luxury, hope of happiness, deliverance from different evils, etc.).

Further, the purely conceptual content of an action is to be regarded as yet another kind of motive. This content has no reference, like the idea of one's own pleasure, solely to the particular action, but to the deduction of an action from a system of moral principles. These moral principles, in the form of abstract concepts, may guide the individual's moral life without his worrying himself about the origin of his concepts. In that case, we feel merely the moral necessity of submitting to a moral concept which, in the form of law, controls our actions. The justification of this necessity we leave to those who demand from us moral subjection, that is, to those whose moral authority over us we acknowledge (the head of the family, the state, social custom, the authority of the church, divine revelation). We meet with a special kind of these moral principles when the law is not proclaimed to us by an external authority, but comes from our own selves (moral autonomy). In this case we believe that we hear the voice, to which we have to submit ourselves, in our own souls. The name for this voice is conscience.

It is a great moral advance when a man no longer takes as the motive of his action the commands of an external or internal authority, but tries to understand the reason why a given maxim of action ought to be effective as a motive in him. This is the advance from morality based on authority to action from moral insight. At this level of morality, a man will try to discover the demands of the moral life, and will let his action be determined by this knowledge. Such demands are (1) the greatest possible happiness of humanity as a whole purely for its own sake, (2) the progress of civilisation, or the moral development of mankind towards ever greater perfection, (3) the realisation of individual moral ends conceived by an act of pure intuition.

The greatest possible happiness of humanity as a whole will naturally be differently conceived by different people. The above-mentioned maxim does not imply any definite idea of this happiness, but rather means that every one who acknowledges this principle strives to do all that, in his opinion, most promotes the good of the whole of humanity.

The progress of civilisation is seen to be a special application of the moral principle just mentioned, at any rate for those to whom the goods which civilisation produces bring feelings of pleasure. However, they will have to pay the price of progress in the destruction and annihilation of many things which also contribute to the happiness of humanity. It is, however, also possible that some men look upon the progress of civilisation as a moral necessity, quite apart from the feelings of pleasure which it brings. If so, the progress of civilisation will be a new moral principle for them, different from the previous one.

Both the principle of the public good, and that of the progress of civilisation, alike depend on the way in which we apply the content of our moral ideas to particular experiences (percepts). The highest principle of morality which we can conceive, however, is that which contains, to start with, no such reference to particular experiences, but which springs from the source of pure intuition and does not seek until later any connection with percepts, *i.e.*, with life. The determination of what ought to be willed issues here from a point of view very different from that of the previous two principles. Whoever accepts the principle of the public good will in all his actions ask first what his ideals contribute to this public good. The upholder of the progress of civilisation as the principle of morality will act similarly. There is, however, a still higher mode of conduct which, in a given case, does not start from any single limited moral ideal, but which sees a certain value in all moral principles, always asking whether this or that principle is more important in a particular case. It may happen that a man considers in certain circumstances the promotion of the public good, in others that of the progress of civilisation, and in yet others the furthering of his own private good, to be the right course, and makes that the motive of his action. But when all other grounds of determination take second place, then we rely, in the first place, on conceptual intuition itself. All other motives now drop out of sight, and the ideal content of an action alone becomes its motive.

Among the levels of characterological disposition, we have singled out as the highest that which manifests itself as pure thought, or practical reason. Among the motives, we have just singled out conceptual intuition as the highest. On nearer consideration, we now perceive that at this level of morality the spring of action and the motive coincide, *i.e.*, that neither a predetermined characterological disposition, nor an external moral principle accepted on authority, influence our conduct. The action, therefore, is neither a merely stereotyped one which follows the rules of a moral code, nor is it automatically performed in response to an external impulse. Rather it is determined solely through its ideal content.

For such an action to be possible, we must first be capable of moral intuitions. Whoever lacks the capacity to think out for himself the moral principles that apply in each particular case, will never rise to the level of genuine individual willing.

Kant's principle of morality: Act so that the principle of your action may be valid for all men—is the exact opposite of ours. His principle would mean death to all individual action. The norm for me can never be what all men would do, but rather what it is right for me to do in each special case.

A superficial criticism might urge against these arguments: How can an action be individually adapted to the special case and the special situation, and yet at the same time be ideally determined by pure intuition? This objection rests on a confusion of the moral motive with the perceptual content of an action. The latter, indeed, may be a motive, and is actually a motive when we act for the progress of culture, or from pure egoism, etc., but in action based on pure moral intuition it never is a motive. Of course, my Self takes notice of these perceptual contents, but it does not allow itself to be determined by them. The content is used only to construct a theoretical concept, but the corresponding moral concept is not derived from the object. The theoretical concept of a given situation which faces me, is a moral concept also only if I adopt the standpoint of a particular moral principle. If I base all my conduct on the principle of the progress of civilisation, then my way through life is tied down to a fixed route. From every occurrence which comes to my notice and attracts my interest there springs a moral duty, viz., to do my tiny share towards using this occurrence in the service of the progress of civilisation. In addition to the concept which reveals to me the connections of events or objects according to the laws of nature, there is also a moral label attached to them which contains for me, as a moral agent, ethical directions as to how I have to conduct myself. At a higher level these moral labels disappear, and my action is determined in each particular instance by my idea; and more particularly by the idea which is suggested to me by the concrete instance.

Men vary greatly in their capacity for intuition. In some, ideas bubble up like a spring, others acquire them with much labour. The situations in which men live, and which are the scenes of their actions, are no less widely different. The conduct of a man will depend, therefore, on the manner in which his faculty of intuition reacts to a given situation. The aggregate of the ideas which are effective in us, the concrete content of our intuitions, constitute that which is individual in each of us, notwithstanding the universal character of our ideas. In so far as this intuitive content has reference to action, it constitutes the moral substance of the individual. To let this substance express itself in his life is the moral principle of the man who regards all other moral principles as subordinate. We may call this point of view Ethical Individualism.

The determining factor of an action, in any concrete instance, is the discovery of the corresponding purely individual intuition. At this level of morality, there can be no question of general moral concepts (norms, laws). General norms always presuppose concrete facts from which they can be deduced. But facts have first to be created by human action.

When we look for the regulating principles (the conceptual principles guiding the actions of individuals, peoples, epochs), we obtain a system of Ethics which is not a science of moral norms, but rather a science of morality as a natural fact. Only the laws discovered in this way are related to human action as the laws of nature are related to particular phenomena. These laws, however, are very far from being identical with the impulses on which we base our actions. If we want to understand how man's moral will gives rise to an action, we must first study the relation of this will to the action. For this purpose we must single out for study those actions in which this relation is the determining factor. When I, or another, subsequently review my action we may discover what moral principles come into play in it. But so long as I am acting, I am influenced, not by these moral principles, but by my love for the object which I want to realise through my action. I ask no man and no moral code, whether I shall perform this action or not. On the contrary, I carry it out as soon as I have formed the idea of it. This alone makes it my action. If a man acts because he accepts certain moral norms, his action is the outcome of the principles which compose his moral code. He merely carries out orders. He is a superior kind of automaton. Inject some stimulus to action into his mind, and at once the clock-work of his moral principles will begin to work and run its prescribed course, so as to issue in an action which is Christian, or humane, or unselfish, or calculated to promote the progress of culture. It is only when I follow solely my love for the object, that it is I, myself, who act. At this level of morality, I acknowledge no lord over me, neither an external authority, nor the so-called voice of my conscience. I acknowledge no external principle of my action, because I have found in myself the ground for my action, viz., my love of the action. I do not ask whether my action is good or bad; I perform it, because I am in love with it. My action is "good" when, with loving intuition, I insert myself in the right way into the world-nexus as I experience it intuitively; it is "bad" when this is not the case. Neither do I ask myself how another man would act in my position. On the contrary, I act as I, this unique individuality, will to act. No general usage, no common custom, no general maxim current among men, no moral norm guides me, but my love for the action. I feel no compulsion, neither the compulsion of nature which dominates me through my instincts, nor the compulsion of the moral commandments. My will is simply to realise what in me lies.

Those who hold to general moral norms will reply to these arguments that, if every one has the right to live himself out and to do what he pleases, there can be no distinction between a good and a bad action; every fraudulent impulse in me has the same right to issue in action as the intention to serve the general good. It is not the mere fact of my having conceived the idea of an action which ought to determine me as a moral agent, but the further examination of whether it is a good or an evil action. Only if it is good ought I to carry it out.

This objection is easily intelligible, and yet it had its root in what is but a misapprehension of my meaning. My reply to it is this: If we want to get at the essence of human volition, we must distinguish between the path along which volition attains to a certain degree of development, and the unique character which it assumes as it approaches its goal. It is on the path towards the goal that the norms play a legitimate part. The goal consists in the realisation of moral aims which are apprehended by pure intuition. Man attains such aims in proportion as he is able to rise at all to the level at which intuition grasps the ideal content of the world. In any particular volition, other elements will, as a rule, be mixed up, as motives or springs of action, with such moral aims. But, for all that, intuition may be, wholly or in part, the determining factor in human volition. What we ought to do, that we do. We supply the stage upon which duty becomes deed. It is our own action which, as such, issues from us. The impulse, then, can only be wholly individual. And, in fact, only a volition which issues out of intuition can be individual. It is only in an age in which immature men regard the blind instincts as part of a man's individuality, that the act of a criminal can be described as living out one's individuality in the same sense, in which the embodiment in action of a pure intuition can be so described.

The animal instinct which drives a man to a criminal act does not spring from intuition, and does not belong to what is individual in him, but rather to that which is most general in him, to that which is equally present in all individuals. The individual element in me is not my organism with its instincts and feelings, but rather the unified world of ideas which reveals itself through this organism. My instincts, cravings, passions, justify no further assertion about me than that I belong to the general species man. The fact that something ideal expresses itself in its own unique way through these instincts, passions, and feelings, constitutes my individuality. My instincts and cravings make me the sort of man of whom there are twelve to the dozen. The unique character of the idea, by means of which I distinguish myself within the dozen as "I," makes of me an individual. Only a being other than myself could distinguish me from others by the difference in my animal nature. By thought, *i.e.*, by the active grasping of the ideal element working itself out through my organism, I distinguish myself from others. Hence it is impossible to say of the action of a criminal that it issues from the idea within him. Indeed, the characteristic feature of criminal actions is precisely that they spring from the non-ideal elements in man.

An act the grounds for which lie in the ideal part of my individual nature is free. Every other act, whether done under the compulsion of nature or under the obligation imposed by a moral norm, is unfree.

That man alone is free who in every moment of his life is able to obey only himself. A moral act is my act only when it can be called free in this sense. So far we are concerned here with the presuppositions under which an act of will is felt to be free; the sequel will show how this purely ethical concept of freedom is realised in the essential nature of man.

Action on the basis of freedom does not exclude, but include, the moral laws. It only shows that it stands on a higher level than actions which are dictated by these laws. Why should my act serve the general good less well when I do it from pure love of it, than when I perform it because it is a duty to serve the general good? The concept of duty excludes freedom, because it will not acknowledge the right of individuality, but demands the subjection of individuality to a general norm. Freedom of action is conceivable only from the standpoint of Ethical Individualism.

But how about the possibility of social life for men, if each aims only at asserting his own individuality? This question expresses yet another objection on the part of Moralism wrongly understood. The Moralist believes that a social community is possible only if all men are held together by a common moral order. This shows that the Moralist does not understand the community of the world of ideas. He does not realise that the world of ideas which inspires me is no other than that which inspires my fellow-men. This identity is, indeed, but a conclusion from our experience of the world. However, it cannot be anything else. For if we could recognise it in any other way than by observation, it would follow that universal norms, not individual experience, were dominant in its sphere. Individuality is possible only if every individual knows others only through individual observation. I differ from my neighbour, not at all because we are living in two entirely different mental worlds, but because from our common world of ideas we receive different intuitions. He desires to live out his intuitions, I mine. If we both draw our intuitions really from the world of ideas, and do not obey mere external impulses (physical or moral), then we cannot but meet one another in striving for the same aims, in having the same intentions. A moral misunderstanding, a clash of aims, is impossible between men who are free. Only the morally unfree who blindly follow their natural instincts or the commands of duty, turn their backs on their neighbours, if these do not obey the same instincts and the same laws as themselves. To live in love of action and to let live in understanding of the other's volition, this is the fundamental maxim of the free man. He knows no other "ought" than that with which his will intuitively puts itself in harmony. How he shall will in any given case, that will be determined for him by the range of his ideas.

If sociability were not deeply rooted in human nature, no external laws would be able to inoculate us with it. It is only because human individuals are akin in spirit that they can live out their lives side by side. The free man lives out his life in the full confidence that all other free men belong to one spiritual world with himself, and that their intentions will coincide with his. The free man does not demand agreement from his fellow-men, but he expects it none the less, believing that it is inherent in human nature. I am not referring here to the necessity for this or that external institution. I refer to the disposition, to the state of mind, through which a man, aware of himself as one of a group of fellow-men for whom he cares, comes nearest to living up to the ideal of human dignity.

There are many who will say that the concept of the free man which I have here developed, is a chimera nowhere to be found realised, and that we have got to deal with actual human beings, from whom we can expect morality only if they obey some moral law, *i.e.*, if they regard their moral task as a duty and do not simply follow their inclinations and loves. I do not deny this. Only a blind man could do that. But, if so, away with all this hypocrisy of morality! Let us say simply that human nature must be compelled to act as long as it is not free. Whether the compulsion of man's unfree nature is effected by physical force or through moral laws, whether man is unfree because he indulges his unmeasured sexual desire, or because he is bound tight in the bonds of conventional morality, is quite immaterial. Only let us not assert that such a man can rightly call his actions his own, seeing that he is driven to them by an external force. But in the midst of all this network of compulsion, there arise free spirits who, in all the welter of customs, legal codes, religious observances, etc., learn to be true to themselves. They are free in so far as they obey only themselves; unfree in so far as they submit to control. Which of us can say that he is really free in all his actions? Yet in each of us there dwells something deeper in which the free man finds expression.

Our life is made up of free and unfree actions. We cannot, however, form a final and adequate concept of human nature without coming upon the free spirit as its purest expression. After all, we are men in the fullest sense only in so far as we are free.

This is an ideal, many will say. Doubtless; but it is an ideal which is a real element in us working up to the surface of our nature. It is no ideal born of mere imagination or dream, but one which has life, and which manifests itself clearly even in the least developed form of its existence. If men were nothing but natural objects, the search for ideals, that is, for ideas which as yet are not actual but the realisation of which we demand, would be an impossibility. In dealing with external objects the idea is determined by the percept. We have done our share when we have recognised the connection between idea and percept. But with a human being the case is different. The content of his existence is not determined without him. His concept of his true self as a moral being (free spirit) is not *a priori* united objectively with the perceptual content "man," so that knowledge need only register the fact subsequently. Man must by his own act unite his concept with the percept "man." Concept and percept coincide with one another in this instance, only in so far as the individual himself makes them coincide. This he can do only if he has found the concept of the free spirit, that is, if he has found the concept of his own Self. In the objective world, a boundary-line is drawn by our organisation between percept and concept. Knowledge breaks down this barrier. In our subjective nature this barrier is no less present. The individual overcomes it in the course of his development, by embodying his concept of himself in his outward existence. Hence man's moral life and his intellectual life lead him both alike to his two-fold nature, perception (immediate experience) and thought. The intellectual life overcomes his two-fold nature by means of knowledge, the moral life succeeds through the actual realisation of the free spirit. Every being has its inborn concept (the laws of its being and action), but in external objects this concept is indissolubly bound up with the percept, and separated from it only in the organisation of human minds. In human beings concept and percept are, at first, actually separated, to be just as actually reunited by them. Someone might object that to our percept of a man there corresponds at every moment of his life a definite concept, just as with external objects. I can construct for myself the concept of an average man, and I may also have given to me a percept to fit this pattern. Suppose now I add to this the concept of a free spirit, then I have two concepts for the same object.

Such an objection is one-sided. As object of perception I am subject to perpetual change. As a child I was one thing, another as a youth, yet another as a man. Moreover, at every moment I am different, as percept, from what I was the moment before. These changes may take place in such a way that either it is always only the same (average) man who exhibits himself in them, or that they represent the expression of a free spirit. Such are the changes which my actions, as objects of perception, undergo.

In the perceptual object "man" there is given the possibility of transformation, just as in the plant-seed there lies the possibility of growth into a fully developed plant. The plant transforms itself in growth, because of the objective law of nature which is inherent in it. The human being remains in his undeveloped state, unless he takes hold of the material for transformation within him and develops himself through his own energy. Nature makes of man merely a natural being; Society makes of him a being who acts in obedience to law; only he himself can make a free man of himself. At a definite stage in his development Nature releases man from her fetters; Society carries his development a step further; he alone can give himself the final polish.

The theory of free morality, then, does not assert that the free spirit is the only form in which man can exist. It looks upon the freedom of the spirit only as the last stage in man's evolution. This is not to deny that conduct in obedience to norms has its legitimate place as a stage in development. The point is that we cannot acknowledge it to be the absolute standpoint in morality. For the free spirit transcends norms, in the sense that he is insensible to them as commands, but regulates his conduct in accordance with his impulses (intuitions).

When Kant apostrophises duty: "Duty! Thou sublime and mighty name, that dost embrace nothing charming or insinuating, but requirest submission," thou that "holdest forth a law ... before which all inclinations are dumb, even though they secretly counterwork it,"[4] then the free spirit replies: "Freedom! thou kindly and humane name, which dost embrace within thyself all that is morally most charming, all that insinuates itself most into my humanity, and which makest me the servant of nobody, which holdest forth no law, but waitest what my inclination itself will proclaim as law, because it resists every law that is forced upon it."

This is the contrast of morality according to law and according to freedom.

The philistine who looks upon the State as embodied morality is sure to look upon the free spirit as a danger to the State. But that is only because his view is narrowly focused on a limited period of time. If he were able to look beyond, he would soon find that it is but on rare occasions that the free spirit needs to go beyond the laws of his state, and that it never needs to confront them with any real contradiction. For the laws of the state, one and all, have had their origin in the intuitions of free spirits, just like all other objective laws of morality. There is no traditional law enforced by the authority of a family, which was not, once upon a time, intuitively conceived and laid down by an ancestor. Similarly the conventional laws of morality are first of all established by particular men, and the laws of the state are always born in the brain of a statesman. These free spirits have set up laws over the rest of mankind, and only he is unfree who forgets this origin and makes them either divine commands, or objective moral duties, or—falsely mystical—the authoritative voice of his own conscience.

He, on the other hand, who does not forget the origin of laws, but looks for it in man, will respect them as belonging to the same world of ideas which is the source also of his own moral intuitions. If he thinks his intuitions better than the existing laws, he will try to put them into the place of the latter. If he thinks the laws justified, he will act in accordance with them as if they were his own intuitions.

Man does not exist in order to found a moral order of the world. Anyone who maintains that he does, stands in his theory of man still at that same point, at which natural science stood when it believed that a bull has horns in order that it may butt. Scientists, happily, have cast the concept of objective purposes in nature into the limbo of dead theories. For Ethics, it is more difficult to achieve the same emancipation. But just as horns do not exist for the sake of butting, but butting because of horns, so man does not exist for the sake of morality, but morality exists through man. The free man acts morally because he has a moral idea, he does not act in order to be moral. Human individuals are the presupposition of a moral world order.

The human individual is the fountain of all morality and the centre of all life. State and society exist only because they have necessarily grown out of the life of individuals. That state and society, in turn, should react upon the lives of individuals, is no more difficult to comprehend, than that the butting which is the result of the existence of horns, reacts in turn upon the further development of the horns, which would become atrophied by prolonged disuse. Similarly, the individual must degenerate if he leads an isolated existence beyond the pale of human society. That is just the reason why the social order arises, viz., that it may react favourably upon the individual.

1

The way in which the above view has influenced psychology, physiology, etc., in various directions has been set forth by the author in works published after this book. Here he is concerned only with characterising the results of an open-minded study of thinking itself.

2

The passage from page 146 down to this point has been added, or rewritten, for the present Revised Edition. (1918).

3

A complete catalogue of the principles of morality (from the point of view of Metaphysical Realism) may be found in Eduard von Hartmann's *Phänomenologie des sittlichen Bewusstseins.*

4

Translation by Abbott, *Kant's Theory of Ethics*, p. 180; *Critique of Pure Practical Reason*, chap. iii.

X

MONISM AND THE PHILOSOPHY OF SPIRITUAL ACTIVITY

The naïve man who acknowledges nothing as real except what he can see with his eyes and grasp with his hands, demands for his moral life, too, grounds of action which are perceptible to his senses. He wants some one who will impart to him these grounds of action in a manner that his senses can apprehend. He is ready to allow these grounds of action to be dictated to him as commands by anyone whom he considers wiser or more powerful than himself, or whom he acknowledges, for whatever reason, to be a power superior to himself. This accounts for the moral principles enumerated above, viz., the principles which rest on the authority of family, state, society, church, and God. The most narrow-minded man still submits to the authority of some single fellow-man. He who is a little more progressive allows his moral conduct to be dictated by a majority (state, society). In every case he relies on some power which is present to his senses. When, at last, the conviction dawns on someone that his authorities are, at bottom, human beings just as weak as himself, then he seeks refuge with a higher power, with a Divine Being, whom, in turn, he endows with qualities perceptible to the senses. He conceives this Being as communicating to him the ideal content of his moral life by way of his senses—believing, for example, that God appears in the flaming bush, or that He moves about among men in manifest human shape, and that their ears can hear His voice telling them what they are to do and what not to do.

The highest stage of development which Naïve Realism attains in the sphere of morality is that at which the moral law (the moral idea) is conceived as having no connection with any external being, but, hypothetically, as being an absolute power in one's own consciousness. What man first listened to as the voice of God, to that he now listens as an independent power in his own mind which he calls conscience. This conception, however, takes us already beyond the level of the naïve consciousness into the sphere where moral laws are treated as independent norms. They are there no longer made dependent on a human mind, but are turned into self-existent metaphysical entities. They are analogous to the visible-invisible forces of Metaphysical Realism. Hence also they appear always as a corollary of Metaphysical Realism, which seeks reality, not in the part which human nature, through its thinking, plays in making reality what it is, but which hypothetically posits reality over and above the facts of experience. Hence these extra-human moral norms always appear as corollaries of Metaphysical Realism. For this theory is bound to look for the origin of morality likewise in the sphere of extra-human reality. There are different possible views of its origin. If the thing-in-itself is unthinking and acts according to purely mechanical laws, as modern Materialism conceives that it does, then it must also produce out of itself, by purely mechanical necessity, the human individual and all that belongs to him. On that view the consciousness of freedom can be nothing more than an illusion. For whilst I consider myself the author of my action, it is the matter of which I am composed and the movements which are going on in it that determine me. I imagine myself free, but actually all my actions are nothing but the effects of the metabolism which is the basis of my physical and mental organisation. It is only because we do not know the motives which compel us that we have the feeling of freedom. "We must emphasise that the feeling of freedom depends on the absence of external compelling motives." "Our actions are as much subject to necessity as our thoughts" (Ziehen, *Leitfaden der Physiologischen Psychologie*, pp. 207, ff.).[1]

Another possibility is that some one will find in a spiritual being the Absolute lying behind all phenomena. If so, he will look for the spring of action in some kind of spiritual power. He will regard the moral principles which his reason contains as the manifestation of this spiritual being, which pursues in men its own special purposes. Moral laws appear to the Dualist, who holds this view, as dictated by the Absolute, and man's only task is to discover, by means of his reason, the decisions of the Absolute and to carry them out. For the Dualist, the moral order of the world is the visible symbol of the higher order that lies behind it. Our human morality is a revelation of the divine world-order. It is not man who matters in this moral order but reality in itself, that is, God. Man ought to do what God wills. Eduard von

Hartmann, who identifies reality, as such, with God, and who treats God's existence as a life of suffering, believes that the Divine Being has created the world in order to gain, by means of the world, release from his infinite suffering. Hence this philosopher regards the moral evolution of humanity as a process, the function of which is the redemption of God. "Only through the building up of a moral world-order on the part of rational, self-conscious individuals is it possible for the world-process to approximate to its goal." "Real existence is the incarnation of God. The world-process is the passion of God who has become flesh, and at the same time the way of redemption for Him who was crucified in the flesh; and morality is our co-operation in the shortening of this process of suffering and redemption" (Hartmann, *Phänomenologie des sittlichen Bewusstseins*, § 871). On this view, man does not act because he wills, but he must act because it is God's will to be redeemed. Whereas the Materialistic Dualist turns man into an automaton, the action of which is nothing but the effect of causality according to purely mechanical laws, the Spiritualistic Dualist (*i.e.*, he who treats the Absolute, the thing-in-itself, as a spiritual something in which man with his conscious experience has no share), makes man the slave of the will of the Absolute. Neither Materialism, nor Spiritualism, nor in general Metaphysical Realism which infers, as true reality, an extra-human something which it does not experience, have any room for freedom.

Naïve and Metaphysical Realism, if they are to be consistent, have to deny freedom for one and the same reason, viz., because, for them, man does nothing but carry out, or execute, principles necessarily imposed upon him. Naïve Realism destroys freedom by subjecting man to authority, whether it be that of a perceptible being, or that of a being conceived on the analogy of perceptible beings, or, lastly, that of the abstract voice of conscience. The Metaphysician, content merely to infer an extra-human reality, is unable to acknowledge freedom because, for him, man is determined, mechanically or morally, by a "thing-in-itself."

Monism will have to admit the partial justification of Naïve Realism, with which it agrees in admitting the part played by the world of percepts. He who is incapable of producing moral ideas through intuition must receive them from others. In so far as a man receives his moral principles from without he is actually unfree. But Monism ascribes to the idea the same importance as to the percept. The idea can manifest itself only in human individuals. In so far as man obeys the impulses coming from this side he is free. But Monism denies all justification to Metaphysics, and consequently also to the impulses of action which are derived from so-called "things-in-themselves." According to the Monistic view, man's action is unfree when he obeys some perceptible external compulsion; it is free when he obeys none but himself. There is no room in Monism for any kind of unconscious compulsion hidden behind percept and concept. If anybody maintains of the action of a fellow-man that it has not been freely done, he is bound to produce within the visible world the thing or the person or the institution which has caused the agent to act. And if he supports his contention by an appeal to causes of action lying outside the real world of our percepts and thoughts, then Monism must decline to take account of such an assertion.

According to the Monistic theory, then, man's action is partly free, partly unfree. He is conscious of himself as unfree in the world of percepts, and he realises in himself the spirit which is free.

The moral laws which his inferences compel the Metaphysician to regard as issuing from a higher power have, according to the upholder of Monism, been conceived by men themselves. To him the moral order is neither a mere image of a purely mechanical order of nature nor of the divine government of the world, but through and through the free creation of men. It is not man's business to realise God's will in the world, but his own. He carries out his own decisions and intentions, not those of another being. Monism does not find behind human agents a ruler of the world, determining them to act according to his will. Men pursue only their own human ends. Moreover, each individual pursues his own private ends. For the world of ideas realises itself, not in a community, but only in individual men. What appears as the common goal of a community is nothing but the result of the separate volitions of its individual members, and most commonly of a few outstanding men whom the rest follow as their leaders. Each one of us has it in him to be a free spirit, just as every rosebud is potentially a rose.

Monism, then, is in the sphere of genuinely moral action the true philosophy of freedom. Being also a philosophy of reality, it rejects the metaphysical (unreal) restriction of the free spirit as emphatically as it acknowledges the physical and historical (naïvely real) restrictions of the naïve man. Inasmuch as it does not look upon man as a finished product, exhibiting in every moment of his life his full nature, it considers idle the dispute whether man, as such, is free or not. It looks upon man as a developing being, and asks whether, in the course of this development, he can reach the stage of the free spirit.

Monism knows that Nature does not send forth man ready-made as a free spirit, but that she leads him up to a certain stage, from which he continues to develop still as an unfree being, until he reaches the point where he finds his own self.

Monism perceives clearly that a being acting under physical or moral compulsion cannot be truly moral. It regards the stages of automatic action (in accordance with natural impulses and instincts), and of obedient action (in accordance with moral norms), as a necessary propædeutic for morality, but it understands that it is possible for the free spirit to transcend both these transitory stages. Monism emancipates man in general from all the self-imposed fetters of the maxims of naïve morality, and from all the externally imposed maxims of speculative Metaphysicians. The former Monism can as little eliminate from the world as it can eliminate percepts. The latter it rejects, because it looks for all principles of explanation of the phenomena of the world within that world and not outside it. Just as Monism refuses even to entertain the thought of cognitive principles other than those applicable to men (p. 125), so it rejects also the concept of moral maxims other than those originated by men. Human morality, like human knowledge, is conditioned by human nature, and just as beings of a higher order would probably mean by knowledge something very different from what we mean by it, so we may assume that other beings would have a very different morality. For Monists, morality is a specifically human quality, and freedom the human way being moral.

1. ADDITION TO THE REVISED EDITION (1918).

In forming a judgment about the argument of the two preceding chapters, a difficulty may arise from what may appear to be a contradiction. On the one side, we have spoken of the experience of thinking as one the significance of which is universal and equally valid for every human consciousness. On the other side, we have pointed out that the ideas which we realise in moral action and which are homogeneous with those that thinking elaborates, manifest themselves in every human consciousness in a uniquely individual way. If we cannot get beyond regarding this antithesis as a "contradiction," and if we do not recognise that in the living intuition of this actually existing antithesis a piece of man's essential nature reveals itself, we shall not be able to apprehend in the true light either what knowledge is or what freedom is. Those who think of concepts as nothing more than abstractions from the world of percepts, and who do not acknowledge the part which intuition plays, cannot but regard as a "pure contradiction" the thought for which we have here claimed reality. But if we understand how ideas are experienced intuitively in their self-sustaining essence, we see clearly that, in knowledge, man lives and enters into the world of ideas as into something which is identical for all men. On the other hand, when man derives from that world the intuitions for his voluntary actions, he individualises a member of the world of ideas by that same activity which he practises as a universally human one in the spiritual and ideal process of cognition. The apparent contradiction between the universal character of cognitive ideas and the individual character of moral ideas becomes, when intuited in its reality, a living concept. It is a criterion of the essential nature of man that what we intuitively apprehend of his nature oscillates, like a living pendulum, between knowledge which is universally valid, and individualised experience of this universal content. Those who fail to perceive the one oscillation in its real character, will regard thinking as a merely subjective human activity. For those who are unable to grasp the other oscillation, man's activity in thinking will seem to lose all individual life. Knowledge is to the former, the moral life to the latter, an unintelligible fact. Both will fall back on all sorts of ideas for the explanation of the one or of the other, because both either do not understand at all how thinking can be intuitively experienced, or, else, misunderstand it as an activity which merely abstracts.

2. Addition to the Revised Edition (1918).

On page 180 I have spoken of Materialism. I am well aware that there are thinkers, like the above-mentioned Th. Ziehen, who do not call themselves Materialists at all, but yet who must be called so from the point of view adopted in this book. It does not matter whether a thinker says that for him the world is not restricted to merely material being, and that, therefore, he is not a Materialist. No, what matters is whether he develops concepts which are applicable only to material being. Anyone who says, "our action, like our thought, is necessarily determined," lays down a concept which is applicable only to material processes, but not applicable either to what we do or to what we are. And if he were to think out what his concept implies, he would end by thinking materialistically. He saves himself from this fate only by the same inconsistency which so often results from not thinking one's thoughts out to the end. It is often said nowadays that the Materialism of the nineteenth century is scientifically dead. But in truth it is not so. It is only that nowadays we frequently fail to notice that we have no other ideas than those which apply only to the material world. Thus recent Materialism is disguised, whereas in the second half of the nineteenth century it openly flaunted itself. Towards a theory which apprehends the world spiritually the camouflaged Materialism of the present is no less intolerant than the self-confessed Materialism of the last century. But it deceives many who think they have a right to reject a theory of the world in terms of Spirit, on the ground that the scientific world-view "has long ago abandoned Materialism."

1 For the manner in which I have here spoken of "Materialism," and for the justification of so speaking of it, see the *Addition* at the end of this chapter.

XI

WORLD-PURPOSE AND LIFE-PURPOSE

(The Destiny of Man)

Among the manifold currents in the spiritual life of humanity there is one which we must now trace, and which we may call the elimination of the concept of purpose from spheres to which it does not belong. Adaptation to purpose is a special kind of sequence of phenomena. Such adaptation is genuinely real only when, in contrast to the relation of cause and effect in which the antecedent event determines the subsequent, the subsequent event determines the antecedent. This is possible only in the sphere of human actions. Man performs actions which he first presents to himself in idea, and he allows himself to be determined to action by this idea. The consequent, *i.e.*, the action, influences by means of the idea the antecedent, *i.e.*, the human agent. If the sequence is to have purposive character, it is absolutely necessary to have this circuitous process through human ideas.

In the process which we can analyse into cause and effect, we must distinguish percept from concept. The percept of the cause precedes the percept of the effect. Cause and effect would simply stand side by side in our consciousness, if we were not able to connect them with one another through the corresponding concepts. The percept of the effect must always be consequent upon the percept of the cause. If the effect is to have a real influence upon the cause, it can do so only by means of the conceptual factor. For the perceptual factor of the effect simply does not exist prior to the perceptual factor of the cause. Whoever maintains that the flower is the purpose of the root, *i.e.*, that the former determines the latter, can make good this assertion only concerning that factor in the flower which his thought reveals in it. The perceptual factor of the flower is not yet in existence at the time when the root originates.

In order to have a purposive connection, it is not only necessary to have an ideal connection of consequent and antecedent according to law, but the concept (law) of the effect must really, *i.e.*, by means of a perceptible process, influence the cause. Such a perceptible influence of a concept upon something else is to be observed only in human actions. Hence this is the only sphere in which the concept of purpose is applicable. The naïve consciousness, which regards as real only what is perceptible, attempts, as we have repeatedly pointed out, to introduce perceptible factors even where only ideal factors can actually be found. In sequences of perceptible events it looks for perceptible connections, or, failing to find them, it imports them by imagination. The concept of purpose, valid for subjective actions, is very convenient for inventing such imaginary connections. The naïve mind knows how it produces events itself, and consequently concludes that Nature proceeds likewise. In the connections of Nature which are purely ideal it finds, not only invisible forces, but also invisible real purposes. Man makes his tools to suit his purposes. On the same principle, so the Naïve Realist imagines, the Creator constructs all organisms. It is but slowly that this mistaken concept of purpose is being driven out of the sciences. In philosophy, even at the present day, it still does a good deal of mischief. Philosophers still ask such questions as, What is the purpose of the world? What is the function (and consequently the purpose) of man? etc.

Monism rejects the concept of purpose in every sphere, with the sole exception of human action. It looks for laws of Nature, but not for purposes of Nature. Purposes of Nature, no less than invisible forces (p. 118), are arbitrary assumptions. But even life-purposes which man does not set up for himself, are, from the standpoint of Monism, illegitimate assumptions. Nothing is purposive except what man has made so, for only the realisation of ideas originates anything purposive. But an idea becomes effective, in the realistic sense, only in human actions. Hence life has no other purpose or function than the one which man gives to it. If the question be asked, What is man's purpose in life? Monism has but one answer: The purpose which he gives to himself. I have no predestined mission in the world; my mission, at any one moment, is that which I choose for myself. I do not enter upon life's voyage with a fixed route mapped out for me.

Ideas are realised only by human agents. Consequently, it is illegitimate to speak of the embodiment of ideas by history. All such statements as "history is the evolution of man towards freedom," or "the realisation of the moral world-order," etc., are, from a Monistic point of view, untenable.

The supporters of the concept of purpose believe that, in surrendering it, they are forced to surrender also all unity and order in the world. Listen, for example, to Robert Hamerling (*Atomistik des Willens*, vol. ii, p. 201): "As long as there are instincts in Nature, so long is it foolish to deny purposes in Nature. Just as the structure of a limb of the human body is not determined and conditioned by an idea of this limb, floating somewhere in mid-air, but by its connection with the more inclusive whole, the body, to which the limb belongs, so the structure of every natural object, be it plant, animal, or man, is not determined and conditioned by an idea of it floating in mid-air, but by the formative principle of the more inclusive whole of Nature which unfolds and organises itself in a purposive manner." And on page 191 of the same volume we read: "Teleology maintains only that, in spite of the thousand misfits and miseries of this natural life, there is a high degree of adaptation to purpose and plan unmistakable in the formations and developments of Nature—an adaptation, however, which is realised only within the limits of natural laws, and which does not tend to the production of some imaginary fairy-land, in which life would not be confronted by death, growth by decay, with all the more or less unpleasant, but quite unavoidable, intermediary stages between them. When the critics of Teleology oppose a laboriously collected rubbish-heap of partial or complete, imaginary or real, maladaptations to a world full of wonders of purposive adaptation, such as Nature exhibits in all her domains, then I consider this just as amusing——"

What is here meant by purposive adaptation? Nothing but the consonance of percepts within a whole. But, since all percepts are based upon laws (ideas), which we discover by means of thinking, it follows that the orderly coherence of the members of a perceptual whole is nothing more than the ideal (logical) coherence of the members of the ideal whole which is contained in this perceptual whole. To say that an animal or a man is not determined by an idea floating in mid-air is a misleading way of putting it, and the view which the critic attacks loses its apparent absurdity as soon as the phrase is put right. An animal certainly is not determined by an idea floating in mid-air, but it is determined by an idea inborn in it and constituting the law of its nature. It is just because the idea is not external to the natural object, but is operative in it as its very essence, that we cannot speak here of adaptation to purpose. Those who deny that natural objects are determined from without (and it does not matter, in this context, whether it be by an idea floating in mid-air or existing in the mind of a creator of the world), are the very men who ought to admit that such an object is not determined by purpose and plan from without, but by cause and law from within. A machine is produced in accordance with a purpose, if I establish a connection between its parts which is not given in Nature. The purposive character of the combinations which I effect consists just in this, that I embody my idea of the working of the machine in the machine itself. In this way the machine comes into existence as an object of perception embodying a corresponding idea. Natural objects have a very similar character. Whoever calls a thing purposive because its form is in accordance with plan or law may, if he so please, call natural objects also purposive, provided only that he does not confuse this kind of purposiveness with that which belongs to a subjective human action. In order to have a purpose, it is absolutely necessary that the efficient cause should be a concept, more precisely a concept of the effect. But in Nature we can nowhere point to concepts operating as causes. A concept is never anything but the ideal nexus of cause and effect. Causes occur in Nature only in the form of percepts.

Dualism may talk of cosmic and natural purposes. Wherever for our perception there is a nexus of cause and effect according to law, there the Dualist is free to assume that we have but the image of a nexus in which the Absolute has realised its purposes. For Monism, on the other hand, the rejection of an Absolute Reality implies also the rejection of the assumption of purposes in World and Nature.

ADDITION TO THE REVISED EDITION (1918).

No one who, with an open mind, has followed the preceding argument, will come to the conclusion that the author, in rejecting the concept of purpose for extra-human facts, intended to side with those thinkers who reject this concept in order to be able to regard, first, everything outside human action and, next, human action itself, as a purely natural process. Against such misunderstanding the author should be protected by the fact that the process of thinking is in this book represented as a purely spiritual process. The reason for rejecting the concept of purpose even for the spiritual world, so far as it lies outside human action, is that in this world there is revealed something higher than a purpose, such as is realised in human life. And when we characterise as erroneous the attempt to conceive the destiny of the human race as purposive according to the pattern of human purposiveness, we mean that the individual adopts purposes, and that the result of the total activity of humanity is composed of these individual purposes. This result is something higher than its component parts, the purposes of individual men.

XII

MORAL IMAGINATION

(Darwin and Morality)

A free spirit acts according to his impulses, *i.e.*, intuitions, which his thought has selected out of the whole world of his ideas. For an unfree spirit, the reason why he singles out a particular intuition from his world of ideas, in order to make it the basis of an action, lies in the perceptual world which is given to him, *i.e.*, in his past experiences. He recalls, before making a decision, what some one else has done, or recommended as proper in an analogous case, or what God has commanded to be done in such a case, etc., and he acts on these recollections. A free spirit dispenses with these preliminaries. His decision is absolutely original. He cares as little what others have done in such a case as what commands they have laid down. He has purely ideal (logical) reasons which determine him to select a particular concept out of the sum of his concepts, and to realise it in action. But his action will belong to perceptible reality. Consequently, what he achieves will coincide with a definite content of perception. His concept will have to be realised in a concrete particular event. As a concept it will not contain this event as particular. It will refer to the event only in its generic character, just as, in general, a concept is related to a percept, *e.g.*, the concept lion to a particular lion. The link between concept and percept is the idea (*cp.* pp. 104 ff). To the unfree spirit this intermediate link is given from the outset. Motives exist in his consciousness from the first in the form of ideas. Whenever he intends to do anything he acts as he has seen others act, or he obeys the instructions he receives in each separate case. Hence authority is most effective in the form of examples, *i.e.*, in the form of traditional patterns of particular actions handed down for the guidance of the unfree spirit. A Christian models his conduct less on the teaching than on the pattern of the Saviour. Rules have less value for telling men positively what to do than for telling them what to leave undone. Laws take on the form of universal concepts only when they forbid actions, not when they prescribe actions. Laws concerning what we ought to do must be given to the unfree spirit in wholly concrete form. Clean the street in front of your door! Pay your taxes to such and such an amount to the tax-collector! etc. Conceptual form belongs to laws which inhibit actions. Thou shalt not steal! Thou shalt not commit adultery! But these laws, too, influence the unfree spirit only by means of a concrete idea, *e.g.*, the idea of the punishments attached by human authority, or of the pangs of conscience, or of eternal damnation, etc.

Even when the motive to an action exists in universal conceptual form (*e.g.*, Thou shalt do good to thy fellow-men! Thou shalt live so that thou promotest best thy welfare!), there still remains to be found, in the particular case, the concrete idea of the action (the relation of the concept to a content of perception). For a free spirit who is not guided by any model nor by fear of punishment, etc., this translation of the concept into an idea is always necessary.

Concrete ideas are formed by us on the basis of our concepts by means of the imagination. Hence what the free spirit needs in order to realise his concepts, in order to assert himself in the world, is moral imagination. This is the source of the free spirit's action. Only those men, therefore, who are endowed with moral imagination are, properly speaking, morally productive. Those who merely preach morality, *i.e.*, those who merely excogitate moral rules without being able to condense them into concrete ideas, are morally unproductive. They are like those critics who can explain very competently how a work of art ought to be made, but who are themselves incapable of the smallest artistic production.

Moral imagination, in order to realise its ideas, must enter into a determinate sphere of percepts. Human action does not create percepts, but transforms already existing percepts and gives them a new character. In order to be able to transform a definite object of perception, or a sum of such objects, in accordance with a moral idea, it is necessary to understand the object's law (its mode of action which one intends to transform, or to which one wants to give a new direction). Further, it is necessary to discover the procedure by which it is possible to change the given law into the new one. This part of effective moral activity depends on knowledge of the particular world of phenomena with which one has got to deal. We shall, therefore, find it in some branch of scientific knowledge. Moral action, then, presupposes, in addition to the faculty of moral concepts[1] and of moral imagination, the ability to alter the world of percepts without violating the natural laws by which they are connected. This ability is moral technique. It may be learnt in the same sense in which science in general may be learnt. For, in general, men are better able to find concepts for the world as it is, than productively to originate out of their imaginations future, and as yet non-existing, actions. Hence, it is very well possible for men without moral imagination to receive moral ideas from others, and to embody these skilfully in the actual world. *Vice versa*, it may happen that men with moral imagination lack technical skill, and are dependent on the service of other men for the realisation of their ideas.

In so far as we require for moral action knowledge of the objects upon which we are about to act, our action depends upon such knowledge. What we need to know here are the laws of nature. These belong to the Natural Sciences, not to Ethics.

Moral imagination and the faculty of moral concepts can become objects of theory only after they have first been employed by the individual. But, thus regarded, they no longer regulate life, but have already regulated it. They must now be treated as efficient causes, like all other causes (they are purposes only for the subject). The study of them is, as it were, the Natural Science of moral ideas.

Ethics as a Normative Science, over and above this science, is impossible.

Some would maintain the normative character of moral laws at least in the sense that Ethics is to be taken as a kind of dietetic which, from the conditions of the organism's life, deduces general rules, on the basis of which it hopes to give detailed directions to the body (Paulsen, *System der Ethik*). This comparison is mistaken, because our moral life cannot be compared with the life of the organism. The behaviour of the organism occurs without any volition on our part. Its laws are fixed data in our world; hence we can discover them and apply them when discovered. Moral laws, on the other hand, do not exist until we create them. We cannot apply them until we have created them. The error is due to the fact that moral laws are not at every moment new creations, but are handed down by tradition. Those which we take over from our ancestors appear to be given like the natural laws of the organism. But it does not follow that a later generation has the right to apply them in the same way as dietetic rules. For they apply to individuals, and not, like natural laws, to specimens of a genus. Considered as an organism, I am such a generic specimen, and I shall live in accordance with nature if I apply the laws of my genus to my particular case. As a moral agent I am an individual and have my own private laws.[2]

The view here upheld appears to contradict that fundamental doctrine of modern Natural Science which is known as the Theory of Evolution. But it only appears to do so. By evolution we mean the real development of the later out of the earlier in accordance with natural law. In the organic world, evolution means that the later (more perfect) organic forms are real descendants of the earlier (imperfect) forms, and have grown out of them in accordance with natural laws. The upholders of the theory of organic evolution believe that there was once a time on our earth, when we could have observed with our own eyes the gradual evolution of reptiles out of Proto-Amniotes, supposing that we could have been present as men, and had been endowed with a sufficiently long span of life. Similarly, Evolutionists suppose that man could have watched the development of the solar system out of the primordial nebula of the Kant-Laplace hypothesis, if he could have occupied a suitable spot in the world-ether during that infinitely long period. But no Evolutionist will dream of maintaining that he could from his concept of the primordial Amnion deduce that of the reptile with all its qualities, even if he had never seen a reptile. Just as little would it be possible to derive the solar system from the concept of the Kant-Laplace nebula, if this concept of an original nebula had been formed only from the percept of the nebula. In other words, if the Evolutionist is to think consistently, he is bound to maintain that out of earlier phases of evolution later ones really develop; that once the concept of the imperfect and that of the perfect have been given, we can understand the connection. But in no case will he admit that the concept formed from the earlier phases is, in itself, sufficient for deducing from it the later phases. From this it follows for Ethics that, whilst we can understand the connection of later moral concepts with earlier ones, it is not possible to deduce a single new moral idea from earlier ones. The individual, as a moral being, produces his own content. This content, thus produced, is for Ethics a datum, as much as reptiles are a datum for Natural Science. Reptiles have evolved out of the Proto-Amniotes, but the scientist cannot manufacture the concept of reptiles out of the concept of the Proto-Amniotes. Later moral ideas evolve out of the earlier ones, but Ethics cannot manufacture out of the moral principles of an earlier age those of a later one. The confusion is due to the fact that, as scientists, we start with the facts before us, and then make a theory about them, whereas in moral action we first produce the facts ourselves, and then theorise about them. In the evolution of the moral world-order we accomplish what, at a lower level, Nature accomplishes: we alter some part of the perceptual world. Hence the ethical norm cannot straightway be made an object of knowledge, like a law of nature, for it must first be created. Only when that has been done can the norm become an object of knowledge.

But is it not possible to make the old a measure for the new? Is not every man compelled to measure the deliverances of his moral imagination by the standard of traditional moral principles? If he would be truly productive in morality, such measuring is as much an absurdity as it would be an absurdity if one were to measure a new species in nature by an old one and say that reptiles, because they do not agree with the Proto-Amniotes, are an illegitimate (degenerate) species.

Ethical Individualism, then, so far from being in opposition to the theory of evolution, is a direct consequence of it. Haeckel's genealogical tree, from protozoa up to man as an organic being, ought to be capable of being worked out without a breach of natural law, and without a gap in its uniform evolution, up to the individual as a being with a determinate moral nature. But, whilst it is quite true that the moral ideas of the individual have perceptibly grown out of those of his ancestors, it is also true that the individual is morally barren, unless he has moral ideas of his own.

The same Ethical Individualism which I have developed on the basis of the preceding principles, might be equally well developed on the basis of the theory of evolution. The final result would be the same; only the path by which it was reached would be different.

That absolutely new moral ideas should be developed by the moral imagination is for the theory of evolution no more inexplicable than the development of one animal species out of another, provided only that this theory, as a Monistic world-view, rejects, in morality as in science, every transcendent (metaphysical) influence. In doing so, it follows the same principle by which it is guided in seeking the causes of new organic forms in forms already existing, but not in the interference of an extra-mundane God, who produces every new species in accordance with a new creative idea through supernatural interference. Just as Monism has no use for supernatural creative ideas in explaining living organisms, so it is equally impossible for it to derive the moral world-order from causes which do not lie within the world. It cannot admit any continuous supernatural influence upon moral life (divine government of the world from the outside), nor an influence either through a particular act of revelation at a particular moment in history (giving of the ten commandments), or through God's appearance on the earth (Divinity of Christ[3]). Moral processes are, for Monism, natural products like everything else that exists, and their causes must be looked for in nature, *i.e.*, in man, because man is the bearer of morality.

Ethical Individualism, then, is the crown of the edifice that Darwin and Haeckel have erected for Natural Science. It is the theory of evolution applied to the moral life.

Anyone who restricts the concept of the natural from the outset to an artificially limited and narrowed sphere, is easily tempted not to allow any room within it for free individual action. The consistent Evolutionist does not easily fall a prey to such a narrow-minded view. He cannot let the process of evolution terminate with the ape, and acknowledge for man a supernatural origin. Again, he cannot stop short at the organic reactions of man and regard only these as natural. He has to treat also the life of moral self-determination as the continuation of organic life. The Evolutionist, then, in accordance with his fundamental principles, can maintain only that moral action evolves out of the less perfect forms of natural processes. He must leave the characterisation of action, *i.e.*, its determination as free action, to the immediate observation of each agent. All that he maintains is only that men have developed out of non-human ancestors. What the nature of men actually is must be determined by observation of men themselves. The results of this observation cannot possibly contradict the history of evolution. Only the assertion that the results are such as to exclude their being due to a natural world-order would contradict recent developments in the Natural Sciences.[4]

Ethical Individualism, then, has nothing to fear from a Natural Science which understands itself. Observation yields freedom as the characteristic quality of the perfect form of human action. Freedom must be attributed to the human will, in so far as the will realises purely ideal intuitions. For these are not the effects of a necessity acting upon them from without, but are grounded in themselves. When we find that an action embodies such an ideal intuition, we feel it to be free. Freedom consists in this character of an action.

What, then, from the standpoint of nature are we to say of the distinction, already mentioned above (p. 8), between the two statements, "To be free means to be able to do what you will," and "To be able, as you please, to strive or not to strive is the real meaning of the dogma of free will"? Hamerling bases his theory of free will precisely on this distinction, by declaring the first statement to be correct but the second to be an absurd tautology. He says, "I can do what I will, but to say I can will what I will is an empty tautology." Whether I am able to do, *i.e.*, to make real, what I will, *i.e.*, what I have set before myself as my idea of action, that depends on external circumstances and on my technical skill (*cp.* p. 200). To be free means to be able to determine by moral imagination out of oneself those ideas (motives) which lie at the basis of action. Freedom is impossible if anything other than I myself (whether a mechanical process or God) determines my moral ideas. In other words, I am free only when I myself produce these ideas, but not when I am merely able to realise the ideas which another being has implanted in me. A free being is one who can will what he regards as right. Whoever does anything other than what he wills must be impelled to it by motives which do not lie in himself. Such a man is unfree in his action. Accordingly, to be able to will, as you please, what you consider right or wrong means to be free or unfree as you please. This is, of course, just as absurd as to identify freedom with the faculty of doing what one is compelled to will. But this is just what Hamerling maintains when he says, "It is perfectly true that the will is always determined by motives, but it is absurd to say that on this ground it is unfree; for a greater freedom can neither be desired nor conceived than the freedom to realise oneself in proportion to one's own power and strength of will." On the contrary, it is well possible to desire a greater freedom and that a true freedom, viz., the freedom to determine for oneself the motives of one's volitions.

Under certain conditions a man may be induced to abandon the execution of his will; but to allow others to prescribe to him what he shall do—in other words, to will what another and not what he himself regards as right—to this a man will submit only when he does not feel free.

External powers may prevent me from doing what I will, but that is only to condemn me to do nothing or to be unfree. Not until they enslave my spirit, drive my motives out of my head, and put their own motives in the place of mine, do they really aim at making me unfree. That is the reason why the church attacks not only the mere doing, but especially the impure thoughts, *i.e.*, motives of my action. And for the church all those motives are impure which she has not herself authorised. A church does not produce genuine slaves until her priests turn themselves into advisers of consciences, *i.e.*, until the faithful depend upon the church, *i.e.*, upon the confessional, for the motives of their actions.

ADDITION TO REVISED EDITION (1918).

In these chapters I have given an account of how every one may experience in his actions something which makes him aware that his will is free. It is especially important to recognise that we derive the right to call an act of will free from the experience of an ideal intuition realising itself in the act. This can be nothing but a datum of observation, in the sense that we observe the development of human volition in the direction towards the goal of attaining the possibility of just such volition sustained by purely ideal intuition. This attainment is possible because the ideal intuition is effective through nothing but its own self-dependent essence. Where such an intuition is present in the mind, it has not developed itself out of the processes in the organism (*cp.* pp. 146 ff.), but the organic processes have retired to make room for the ideal processes. Observation of an act of will which embodies an intuition shows that out of it, likewise, all organically necessary activity has retired. The act of will is free. No one can observe this freedom of will who is unable to see how free will consists in this, that, first, the intuitive factor lames and represses the necessary activity of the human organism, and then puts in its place the spiritual activity of a will guided by ideas. Only those who are unable to observe these two factors in the free act of will believe that every act of will is unfree. Those who are able to observe them win through to the recognition that man is unfree in so far as he fails to repress organic activity completely, but that this unfreedom is tending towards freedom, and that this freedom, so far from being an abstract ideal, is a directive force inherent in human nature. Man is free in proportion as he succeeds in realising in his acts of will the same disposition of mind, which possesses him when he is conscious in himself of the formation of purely ideal (spiritual) intuitions.

1

Only a superficial critic will find in the use of the word "faculty," in this and other passages, a relapse into the old-fashioned doctrine of faculties of the soul.

2

When Paulsen, p. 15 of the book mentioned above, says: "Different natural endowments and different conditions of life demand both a different bodily and also a different mental and moral diet," he is very close to the correct view, but yet he misses the decisive point. In so far as I am an individual, I need no diet. Dietetic means the art of bringing a particular specimen into harmony with the universal laws of the genus. But as an individual I am not a specimen of a genus.

3

The Editor would call the reader's attention to the fact that this book was written in 1894. For many years Dr. Steiner's efforts have been chiefly concentrated in upholding the Divinity of Christ consistently with the broader lines of the Christian Churches.

4

We are entitled to speak of thoughts (ethical ideas) as objects of observation. For, although the products of thinking do not enter the field of observation, so long as the thinking goes on, they may well become objects of observation subsequently. In this way we have gained our characterisation of action.

XIII

THE VALUE OF LIFE

(Optimism and Pessimism)

A counterpart of the question concerning the purpose and function of life (*cp.* pp. 190 ff.) is the question concerning its value. We meet here with two mutually opposed views, and between them with all conceivable attempts at compromise. One view says that this world is the best conceivable which could exist at all, and that to live and act in it is a good of inestimable value. Everything that exists displays harmonious and purposive co-operation and is worthy of admiration. Even what is apparently bad and evil may, from a higher point of view, be seen to be a good, for it represents an agreeable contrast with the good. We are the more able to appreciate the good when it is clearly contrasted with evil. Moreover, evil is not genuinely real; it is only that we perceive as evil a lesser degree of good. Evil is the absence of good, it has no positive import of its own.

The other view maintains that life is full of misery and agony. Everywhere pain outweighs pleasure, sorrow outweighs joy. Existence is a burden, and non-existence would, from every point of view, be preferable to existence.

The chief representatives of the former view, *i.e.*, Optimism, are Shaftesbury and Leibnitz; the chief representatives of the second, *i.e.*, Pessimism, are Schopenhauer and Eduard von Hartmann.

Leibnitz says the world is the best of all possible worlds. A better one is impossible. For God is good and wise. A good God wills to create the best possible world, a wise God knows which is the best possible. He is able to distinguish the best from all other and worse possibilities. Only an evil or an unwise God would be able to create a world worse than the best possible.

Whoever starts from this point of view will find it easy to lay down the direction which human action must follow, in order to make its contribution to the greatest good of the universe. All that man need do will be to find out the counsels of God and to act in accordance with them. If he knows what

God's purposes are concerning the world and the human race, he will be able, for his part, to do what is right. And he will be happy in the feeling that he is adding his share to all the other good in the world. From this optimistic standpoint, then, life is worth living. It is such as to stimulate us to co-operate with, and enter into, it.

Quite different is the picture Schopenhauer paints. He thinks of ultimate reality not as an all-wise and all-beneficent being, but as blind striving or will. Eternal striving, ceaseless craving for satisfaction which yet is ever beyond reach, these are the fundamental characteristics of all will. For as soon as we have attained what we want, a fresh need springs up, and so on. Satisfaction, when it occurs, endures always only for an infinitesimal time. The whole rest of our lives is unsatisfied craving, *i.e.*, discontent and suffering. When at last blind craving is dulled, every definite content is gone from our lives. Existence is filled with nothing but an endless ennui. Hence the best we can do is to throttle all desires and needs within us and exterminate the will. Schopenhauer's Pessimism leads to complete inactivity; its moral aim is universal idleness.

By a very different argument Von Hartmann attempts to establish Pessimism and to make use of it for Ethics. He attempts, in keeping with the fashion of our age, to base his world-view on experience. By observation of life he hopes to discover whether there is more pain or more pleasure in the world. He passes in review before the tribunal of reason whatever men consider to be happiness and a good, in order to show that all apparent satisfaction turns out, on closer inspection, to be nothing but illusion. It is illusion when we believe that in health, youth, freedom, sufficient income, love (sexual satisfaction), pity, friendship and family life, honour, reputation, glory, power, religious edification, pursuit of science and of art, hope of a life after death, participation in the advancement of civilisation—that in all these we have sources of happiness and satisfaction. Soberly considered, every enjoyment brings much more evil and misery than pleasure into the world. The disagreeableness of "the morning after" is always greater than the agreeableness of intoxication. Pain far outweighs pleasure in the world. No man, even though relatively the happiest, would, if asked, wish to live through this miserable life a second time. Now, since

Hartmann does not deny the presence of an ideal factor (wisdom) in the world, but, on the contrary, grants to it equal rights with blind striving (will), he can attribute the creation of the world to his Absolute Being only on condition that He makes the pain in the world subserve a world-purpose that is wise. But the pain of created beings is nothing but God's pain itself, for the life of Nature as a whole is identical with the life of God. An All-wise Being can aim only at release from pain, and since all existence is pain, at release from existence. Hence the purpose of the creation of the world is to transform existence into the non-existence which is so much better. The world-process is nothing but a continuous battle against God's pain, a battle which ends with the annihilation of all existence. The moral life for men, therefore, will consist in taking part in the annihilation of existence. The reason why God has created the world is that through the world he may free himself from his infinite pain. The world must be regarded, "as it were, as an itching eruption on the Absolute," by means of which the unconscious healing power of the Absolute rids itself of an inward disease; or it may be regarded "as a painful drawing-plaster which the All-One applies to itself in order first to divert the inner pain outwards, and then to get rid of it altogether." Human beings are members of the world. In their sufferings God suffers. He has created them in order to split up in them his infinite pain. The pain which each one of us suffers is but a drop in the infinite ocean of God's pain (Hartmann, *Phänomenologie des Sittlichen Bewusstseins*, pp. 866 ff.).

It is man's duty to permeate his whole being with the recognition that the pursuit of individual satisfaction (Egoism) is a folly, and that he ought to be guided solely by the task of assisting in the redemption of God by unselfish service of the world-process. Thus, in contrast with the Pessimism of Schopenhauer, that of Von Hartmann leads us to devoted activity in a sublime cause.

But what of the claim that this view is based on experience?

To strive after satisfaction means that our activity reaches out beyond the actual content of our lives. A creature is hungry, *i.e.*, it desires satiety, when its organic functions demand for their continuation the supply of fresh life-materials in the form of nourishment. The pursuit of honour consists in that a man does not regard what he personally does or leaves undone as valuable unless it is endorsed by the approval of others from without. The striving for knowledge arises when a man is not content with the world which he sees, hears, etc., so long as he has not understood it. The fulfilment of the striving causes pleasure in the individual who strives, failure causes pain. It is important here to observe that pleasure and pain are attached only to the fulfilment or non-fulfilment of my striving. The striving itself is by no means to be regarded as a pain. Hence, if we find that, in the very moment in which a striving is fulfilled, at once a new striving arises, this is no ground for saying that pleasure has given birth to pain, because enjoyment in every case gives rise to a desire for its repetition, or for a fresh pleasure. I can speak of pain only when desire runs up against the impossibility of fulfilment. Even when an enjoyment that I have had causes in me the desire for the experience of a greater, more subtle, and more exotic pleasure, I have no right to speak of this desire as a pain caused by the previous pleasure until the means fail me to gain the greater and more subtle pleasure. I have no right to regard pleasure as the cause of pain unless pain follows on pleasure as its consequence by natural law, *e.g.*, when a woman's sexual pleasure is followed by the suffering of child-birth and the cares of nursing. If striving caused pain, then the removal of striving ought to be accompanied by pleasure. But the very reverse is true. To have no striving in one's life causes boredom, and boredom is always accompanied by displeasure. Now, since it may be a long time before a striving meets with fulfilment, and since, in the interval, it is content with the hope of fulfilment, we must acknowledge that there is no connection in principle between pain and striving, but that pain depends solely on the non-fulfilment of the striving. Schopenhauer, then, is wrong, in any case, in regarding desire or striving (will) as being in principle the source of pain.

In truth, the very reverse of this is correct. Striving (desire) is in itself pleasurable. Who does not know the pleasure which is caused by the hope of a remote but intensely desired enjoyment? This pleasure is the companion of all labour, the results of which will be enjoyed by us only in the future. It is a pleasure which is wholly independent of the attainment of the end. For when the aim has been attained, the pleasure of satisfaction is added as a fresh thrill to the pleasure of striving. If anyone were to argue that the pain caused by the non-attainment of an aim is increased by the pain of disappointed hope, and that thus, in the end, the pain of non-fulfilment will still always outweigh the utmost possible pleasure of fulfilment, we shall have to reply that the reverse may be the case, and that the recollection of past pleasure at a time of unsatisfied desire will as often mitigate the displeasure of non-satisfaction. Whoever at the moment when his hopes suffer shipwreck exclaims, "I have done my part," proves thereby my assertion. The blessed feeling of having willed the best within one's powers is ignored by all who make every unsatisfied desire an occasion for asserting that, not only has the pleasure of fulfilment been lost, but that the enjoyment of the striving itself has been destroyed.

The satisfaction of a desire causes pleasure and its non-satisfaction causes pain. But we have no right to infer from this fact that pleasure is nothing but the satisfaction of a desire, and pain nothing but its non-satisfaction. Both pleasure and pain may be experienced without being the consequence of desire. All illness is pain not preceded by any desire. If anyone were to maintain that illness is unsatisfied desire for health, he would commit the error of regarding the inevitable and unconscious wish not to fall ill as a positive desire. When some one receives a legacy from a rich relative of whose existence he had not the faintest idea, he experiences a pleasure without having felt any preceding desire.

Hence, if we set out to inquire whether the balance is on the side of pleasure or of pain, we must allow in our calculation for the pleasure of striving, the pleasure of the satisfaction of striving, and the pleasure which comes to us without any striving whatever. On the debit side we shall have to enter the displeasure of boredom, the displeasure of unfulfilled striving, and, lastly, the displeasure which comes to us without any striving on our part. Under this last heading we shall have to put also the displeasure caused by work that has been forced upon us, not chosen by ourselves.

This leads us to the question, What is the right method for striking the balance between the credit and the debit columns? Eduard von Hartmann asserts that reason holds the scales. It is true that he says (*Philosophie des*

Unbewussten, 7th edition, vol. ii. p. 290): "Pain and pleasure exist only in so far as they are actually being felt." It follows that there can be no standard for pleasure other than the subjective standard of feeling. I must feel whether the sum of my disagreeable feelings, contrasted with my agreeable feelings, results in me in a balance of pleasure or of pain. But, notwithstanding this, Von Hartmann maintains that "though the value of the life of every being can be set down only according to its own subjective measure, yet it follows by no means that every being is able to compute the correct algebraic sum of all the feelings of its life—or, in other words, that its total estimate of its own life, with regard to its subjective feelings, should be correct." But this means that rational estimation of feelings is reinstated as the standard of value.[1]

It is because Von Hartmann holds this view that he thinks it necessary, in order to arrive at a correct valuation of life, to clear out of the way those factors which falsify our judgment about the balance of pleasure and of pain. He tries to do this in two ways: first, by showing that our desire (instinct, will) operates as a disturbing factor in the sober estimation of feeling-values; *e.g.*, whereas we ought to judge that sexual enjoyment is a source of evil, we are beguiled by the fact that the sexual instinct is very strong in us, into pretending to experience a pleasure which does not occur in the alleged intensity at all. We are bent on indulging ourselves, hence we do not acknowledge to ourselves that the indulgence makes us suffer. Secondly, Von Hartmann subjects feelings to a criticism designed to show, that the objects to which our feelings attach themselves reveal themselves as illusions when examined by reason, and that our feelings are destroyed from the moment that our constantly growing insight sees through the illusions.

Von Hartmann, then, conceives the matter as follows. Suppose an ambitious man wants to determine clearly whether, up to the moment of his inquiry, there has been a surplus of pleasure or of pain in his life. He has to eliminate two sources of error that may affect his judgment. Being ambitious, this fundamental feature of his character will make him see all the pleasures of the public recognition of his achievements larger than they are, and all the insults suffered through rebuffs smaller than they are. At the time when he suffered the rebuffs he felt the insults just because he is ambitious, but in recollection they appear to him in a milder light, whereas the pleasures of recognition to which he is so much more susceptible leave a far deeper impression. Undeniably, it is a real benefit to an ambitious man that it should be so, for the deception diminishes his pain in the moment of self-analysis. But, none the less, it falsifies his judgments. The sufferings which he now reviews as through a veil were actually experienced by him in all their intensity. Hence he enters them at a wrong valuation on the debit side of his account. In order to arrive at a correct estimate, an ambitious man would have to lay aside his ambition for the time of his inquiry. He would have to review his past life without any distorting glasses before his mind's eye, else he will resemble a merchant who, in making up his books, enters among the items on the credit side his own zeal in business.

But Von Hartmann goes even further. He says the ambitious man must make clear to himself that the public recognition which he craves is not worth having. By himself, or with the guidance of others, he must attain the insight that rational beings cannot attach any value to recognition by others, seeing that "in all matters which are not vital questions of development, or which have not been definitely settled by science," it is always as certain as anything can be "that the majority is wrong and the minority right." "Whoever makes ambition the lode-star of his life puts the happiness of his life at the mercy of so fallible a judgment" (*Philosophie des Unbewussten*, vol. ii, p. 332). If the ambitious man acknowledges all this to himself, he is bound to regard all the achievements of his ambition as illusions, including even the feelings which attach themselves to the satisfaction of his ambitious desires. This is the reason why Von Hartmann says that we must also strike out of the balance-sheet of our life-values whatever is seen to be illusory in our feelings of pleasure. What remains after that represents the sum-total of pleasure in life, and this sum is so small compared with the sum-total of pain that life is no enjoyment and non-existence preferable to existence.

But whilst it is immediately evident that the interference of the instinct of ambition produces self-deception in striking the balance of pleasures and thus leads to a false result, we must none the less challenge what Von

Hartmann says concerning the illusory character of the objects to which pleasure is attached. For the elimination, from the credit-side of life, of all pleasurable feelings which accompany actual or supposed illusions would positively falsify the balance of pleasure and of pain. An ambitious man has genuinely enjoyed the acclamations of the multitude, irrespective of whether subsequently he himself, or some other person, recognises that this acclamation is an illusion. The pleasure, once enjoyed, is not one whit diminished by such recognition. Consequently the elimination of all these "illusory" feelings from life's balance, so far from making our judgment about our feelings more correct, actually cancels out of life feelings which were genuinely there.

And why are these feelings to be eliminated? He who has them derives pleasure from them; he who has overcome them, gains through the experience of self-conquest (not through the vain emotion: What a noble fellow I am! but through the objective sources of pleasure which lie in the self-conquest) a pleasure which is, indeed, spiritualised, but none the less valuable for that. If we strike feelings from the credit side of pleasure in our account, on the ground that they are attached to objects which turn out to have been illusory, we make the value of life dependent, not on the quantity, but on the quality of pleasure, and this, in turn, on the value of the objects which cause the pleasure. But if I am to determine the value of life only by the quantity of pleasure or pain which it brings, I have no right to presuppose something else by which first to determine the positive or negative value of pleasure. If I say I want to compare quantity of pleasure and quantity of pain, in order to see which is greater, I am bound to bring into my account all pleasures and pains in their actual intensities, regardless of whether they are based on illusions or not. If I credit a pleasure which rests on an illusion with a lesser value for life than one which can justify itself before the tribunal of reason, I make the value of life dependent on factors other than mere quantity of pleasure.

Whoever, like Eduard von Hartmann, puts down pleasure as less valuable when it is attached to a worthless object, is like a merchant who enters the considerable profits of a toy-factory at only one-quarter of their real value on the ground that the factory produces nothing but playthings for children.

If the point is simply to weigh quantity of pleasure against quantity of pain, we ought to leave the illusory character of the objects of some pleasures entirely out of account.

The method, then, which Von Hartmann recommends, viz., rational criticism of the quantities of pleasure and pain produced by life, has taught us so far how we are to get the data for our calculation, *i.e.*, what we are to put down on the one side of our account and what on the other. But how are we to make the actual calculation? Is reason able also to strike the balance?

A merchant makes a miscalculation when the gain calculated by him does not balance with the profits which he has demonstrably enjoyed from his business or is still expecting to enjoy. Similarly, the philosopher will undoubtedly have made a mistake in his estimate, if he cannot demonstrate in actual feeling the surplus of pleasure or, as the case may be, of pain which his manipulation of the account may have yielded.

For the present I shall not criticise the calculations of those Pessimists who support their estimate of the value of the world by an appeal to reason. But if we are to decide whether to carry on the business of life or not, we shall demand first to be shown where the alleged balance of pain is to be found.

Here we touch the point where reason is not in a position by itself to determine the surplus of pleasure or of pain, but where it must exhibit this surplus in life as something actually felt. For man reaches reality not through concepts by themselves, but through the interpenetration of concepts and percepts (and feelings are percepts) which thinking brings about (*cp.* pp. 82 ff.). A merchant will give up his business only when the loss of goods, as calculated by his accountant, is actually confirmed by the facts. If the facts do not bear out the calculation, he asks his accountant to check the account once more. That is exactly what a man will do in the business of life. If a philosopher wants to prove to him that the pain is far greater than the pleasure, but that he does not feel it so, then he will reply: "You have made a mistake in your theorisings; repeat your analysis once more." But if there comes a time in a business when the losses are really so great that the firm's credit no longer suffices to satisfy the creditors, bankruptcy results, even though the merchant may avoid keeping himself informed by careful accounts about the state of his affairs. Similarly, supposing the quantity of pain in a man's life became at any time so great that no hope (credit) of future pleasure could help him to get over the pain, the bankruptcy of life's business would inevitably follow.

Now the number of those who commit suicide is relatively small compared with the number of those who live bravely on. Only very few men give up the business of life because of the pain involved. What follows? Either that it is untrue to say that the quantity of pain is greater than the quantity of pleasure, or that we do not make the continuation of life dependent on the quantity of felt pleasure or pain.

In a very curious way, Eduard von Hartmann's Pessimism, having concluded that life is valueless because it contains a surplus of pain, yet affirms the necessity of going on with life. This necessity lies in the fact that the world-purpose mentioned above (p. 216) can be achieved only by the ceaseless, devoted labour of human beings. But so long as men still pursue their egoistical appetites they are unfit for this devoted labour. It is not until experience and reason have convinced them that the pleasures which Egoism pursues are incapable of attainment, that they give themselves up to their proper task. In this way the pessimistic conviction is offered as the fountain of unselfishness. An education based on Pessimism is to exterminate Egoism by convincing it of the hopelessness of achieving its aims.

According to this view, then, the striving for pleasure is fundamentally inherent in human nature. It is only through the insight into the impossibility of satisfaction that this striving abdicates in favour of the higher tasks of humanity.

It is, however, impossible to say of this ethical theory, which expects from the establishment of Pessimism a devotion to unselfish ends in life, that it really overcomes Egoism in the proper sense of the word. The moral ideas are said not to be strong enough to dominate the will until man has learnt that the selfish striving after pleasure cannot lead to any satisfaction. Man, whose selfishness desires the grapes of pleasure, finds them sour because he cannot attain them, and so he turns his back on them and devotes himself to an unselfish life. Moral ideals, then, according to the opinion of Pessimists, are too weak to overcome Egoism, but they establish their kingdom on the territory which previous recognition of the hopelessness of Egoism has cleared for them.

If men by nature strive after pleasure but are unable to attain it, it follows that annihilation of existence and salvation through non-existence are the only rational ends. And if we accept the view that the real bearer of the pain of the world is God, it follows that the task of men consists in helping to bring about the salvation of God. To commit suicide does not advance, but hinders, the realisation of this aim. God must rationally be conceived as having created men for the sole purpose of bringing about his salvation through their action, else would creation be purposeless. Every one of us has to perform his own definite task in the general work of salvation. If he withdraws from the task by suicide, another has to do the work which was intended for him. Somebody else must bear in his stead the agony of existence. And since in every being it is, at bottom, God who is the ultimate bearer of all pain, it follows that to commit suicide does not in the least diminish the quantity of God's pain, but rather imposes upon God the additional difficulty of providing a substitute.

This whole theory presupposes that pleasure is the standard of value for life. Now life manifests itself through a number of instincts (needs). If the value of life depended on its producing more pleasure than pain, an instinct would have to be called valueless which brought to its owner a balance of pain. Let us, if you please, inspect instinct and pleasure, in order to see whether the former can be measured by the latter. And lest we give rise to the suspicion that life does not begin for us below the sphere of the "aristocrats of the intellect," we shall begin our examination with a "purely animal" need, viz., hunger.

Hunger arises when our organs are unable to continue functioning without a fresh supply of food. What a hungry man desires, in the first instance, is to have his hunger stilled. As soon as the supply of nourishment has reached the point where hunger ceases, everything has been attained that the food-instinct craves. The pleasure which is connected with satiety consists, to begin with, in the removal of the pain which is caused by hunger. But to the mere food-instinct there is added a further need. For man does not merely desire to restore, by the consumption of food, the disturbance in the functioning of his organs, or to get rid of the pain of hunger, but he seeks to effect this to the accompaniment of pleasurable sensations of taste. When he feels hungry, and is within half an hour of a meal to which he looks forward with pleasure, he avoids spoiling his enjoyment of the better food by taking inferior food which might satisfy his hunger sooner. He needs hunger in order to get the full enjoyment out of his meal. Thus hunger becomes for him at the same time a cause of pleasure. Supposing all the hunger in the world could be satisfied, we should get the total quantity of pleasure which we owe to the existence of the desire for nourishment. But we should still have to add the additional pleasure which gourmets gain by cultivating the sensibility of their taste-nerves beyond the common measure.

The greatest conceivable value of this quantity of pleasure would be reached, if no need remained unsatisfied which was in any way connected with this kind of pleasure, and if with the smooth of pleasure we had not at the same time to take a certain amount of the rough of pain.

Modern Science holds the view that Nature produces more life than it can maintain, *i.e.*, that Nature also produces more hunger than it is able to satisfy. The surplus of life thus produced is condemned to a painful death in the struggle for existence. Granted that the needs of life are, at every moment of the world-process, greater than the available means of satisfaction, and that the enjoyment of life is correspondingly diminished, yet such enjoyment as actually occurs is not one whit reduced thereby. Wherever a desire is satisfied, there the corresponding quantity of pleasure exists, even though in the creature itself which desires, or in its fellow-creatures, there are a large number of unsatisfied instincts. What is diminished is, not the quantity, but the "value" of the enjoyment of life. If only a part of the needs of a living creature find satisfaction, it experiences still a corresponding pleasure. This pleasure is inferior in value in proportion as it is inadequate to the total demand of life within a given group of desires. We might represent this value as a fraction, the numerator of which is the actually experienced pleasure, whilst the denominator is the sum-total of needs. This fraction has the value 1 when the numerator and the denominator are equal, *i.e.*, when all needs are also satisfied. The fraction becomes greater than 1 when a creature experiences more pleasure than its desires demand. It becomes smaller than 1 when the quantity of pleasure falls short of the sum-total of desires. But the fraction can never have the value 0 so long as the numerator has any value at all, however small. If a man were to make up the account before his death and to distribute in imagination over the whole of life the quantity belonging to a particular instinct (*e.g.*, hunger), as well as the demands of this instinct, then the total pleasure which he has experienced might have only a very small value, but this value would never become altogether nil. If the quantity of pleasure remains constant, then with every increase in the needs of the creature the value of the pleasure diminishes. The same is true for the totality of life in Nature. The greater the number of creatures in proportion to those which are able fully to satisfy their instincts, the smaller is the average pleasure-value of life. The cheques on life's pleasure which are drawn in our favour in the form of our instincts, become increasingly less valuable in proportion as we cannot expect to cash them at their full face value. Suppose I get enough to eat on three days and am then compelled to go hungry for another three days, the actual pleasure on the three days of eating is not thereby diminished. But I have now to think of it as distributed over six days, and this reduces its "value" for my food-instinct by half. The same applies to the quantity of pleasure as measured by the degree of my need. Suppose I have hunger enough for two sandwiches and can only get one, the pleasure which this one gives me has only half the value it would have had if the eating of it had stilled my hunger. This is the way in which we determine the value of a pleasure in life. We determine it by the needs of life. Our desires supply the measure; pleasure is what is measured. The pleasure of stilling hunger has value only because hunger exists, and it has determinate value through the proportion which it bears to the intensity of the hunger.

Unfulfilled demands of our life throw their shadow even upon fulfilled desires, and thus detract from the value of pleasurable hours. But we may speak also of the present value of a feeling of pleasure. This value is the smaller, the more insignificant the pleasure is in proportion to the duration and intensity of our desire.

A quantity of pleasure has its full value for us when its duration and degree exactly coincide with our desire. A quantity of pleasure which is smaller than our desire diminishes the value of the pleasure. A quantity which is greater produces a surplus which has not been demanded and which is felt as pleasure only so long as, whilst enjoying the pleasure, we can correspondingly increase the intensity of our desire. If we are not able to keep pace in the increase of our desire with the increase in pleasure, then pleasure turns into displeasure. The object which would otherwise satisfy us, when it assails us unbidden makes us suffer. This proves that pleasure has value for us only so long as we have desires by which to measure it. An excess of pleasurable feeling turns into pain. This may be observed especially in those men whose desire for a given kind of pleasure is very small. In people whose desire for food is dulled, eating easily produces nausea. This again shows that desire is the measure of value for pleasure.

Now Pessimism might reply that an unsatisfied desire for food produces, not only the pain of a lost enjoyment, but also positive ills, agony, and misery in the world. It appeals for confirmation to the untold misery of all who are harassed by anxieties about food, and to the vast amount of pain which for these unfortunates results indirectly from their lack of food. And if it wants to extend its assertion also to non-human nature, it can point to the agonies of animals which, in certain seasons, die from lack of food. Concerning all these evils the Pessimist maintains that they far outweigh the quantity of pleasure which the food-instinct brings into the world.

There is no doubt that it is possible to compare pleasure and pain one with another, and determine the surplus of the one or the other as we determine commercial gain or loss. But if Pessimists think that a surplus on the side of pain is a ground for inferring that life is valueless, they fall into the mistake of making a calculation which in actual life is never made.

Our desire, in any given case, is directed to a particular object. The value of the pleasure of satisfaction, as we have seen, will be the greater in proportion as the quantity of the pleasure is greater relatively to the intensity of our desire.[2] It depends, further, on this intensity how large a quantity of pain we are willing to bear in order to gain the pleasure. We compare the quantity of pain, not with the quantity of pleasure, but with the intensity of our desire. He who finds great pleasure in eating will, by reason of his pleasure in better times, be more easily able to bear a period of hunger than one who does not derive pleasure from the satisfaction of the instinct for food. A woman who wants a child compares the pleasures resulting from the possession of a child, not with the quantities of pain due to pregnancy, birth, nursing, etc., but with her desire for the possession of the child.

We never aim at a certain quantity of pleasure in the abstract, but at concrete satisfaction of a perfectly determinate kind. When we are aiming at a definite object or a definite sensation, it will not satisfy us to be offered some other object or some other sensation, even though they give the same amount of pleasure. If we desire satisfaction of hunger, we cannot substitute for the pleasure which this satisfaction would bring a pleasure equally great but produced by a walk. Only if our desire were, quite generally, for a certain quantity of pleasure, would it have to die away at once if this pleasure were unattainable except at the price of an even greater quantity of pain. But because we desire a determinate kind of satisfaction, we experience the pleasure of realisation even when, along with it, we have to bear an even greater pain. The instincts of living beings tend in a determinate direction and aim at concrete objects, and it is just for this reason that it is impossible, in our calculations, to set down as an equivalent factor the quantities of pain which we have to bear in the pursuit of our object. Provided the desire is sufficiently intense to be still to some degree in existence even after having overcome the pain—however great that pain, taken in the abstract, may be—the pleasure of satisfaction may still be enjoyed to its full extent. The desire, therefore, does not measure the pain directly against the pleasure which we attain, but indirectly by measuring the pain (proportionately) against its own intensity. The question is not whether the pleasure to be gained is greater than the pain, but whether the desire for the object at which we aim is greater than the inhibitory effect of the pain which we have to face. If the inhibition is greater than the desire, the latter yields to the inevitable, slackens, and ceases to strive. But inasmuch as we strive after a determinate kind of satisfaction, the pleasure we gain thereby acquires an importance which makes it possible, once satisfaction has been attained, to allow in our calculation for the inevitable pain only in so far as it has diminished the intensity of our desire. If I am passionately fond of beautiful views, I never calculate the amount of pleasure which the view from the mountain-top gives me as compared directly with the pain of the toilsome ascent and descent; but I reflect whether, after having overcome all difficulties, my desire for the view will still be sufficiently intense. Thus pleasure and pain can be made commensurate only mediately through the intensity of the desire. Hence the question is not at all whether there is a surplus of pleasure or of pain, but whether the desire for pleasure is sufficiently intense to overcome the pain.

A proof for the accuracy of this view is to be found in the fact, that we put a higher value on pleasure when it has to be purchased at the price of great pain than when it simply falls into our lap like a gift from heaven. When sufferings and agonies have toned down our desire and yet after all our aim is attained, then the pleasure is all the greater in proportion to the intensity of the desire that has survived. Now it is just this proportion which, as I have shown (p. 233), represents the value of the pleasure. A further proof is to be found in the fact that all living creatures (including men) develop their instincts as long as they are able to bear the opposition of pains and agonies. The struggle for existence is but a consequence of this fact. All living creatures strive to expand, and only those abandon the struggle whose desires are throttled by the overwhelming magnitude of the difficulties with which they meet. Every living creature seeks food until sheer lack of food destroys its life. Man, too, does not turn his hand against himself until, rightly or wrongly, he believes that he cannot attain those aims in life which alone seem to him worth striving for. So long as he still believes in the possibility of attaining what he thinks worth striving for, he will battle against all pains and miseries. Philosophy would have to convince man that striving is rational only when pleasure outweighs pain, for it is his nature to strive for the attainment of the objects which he desires, so long as he can bear the inevitable incidental pain, however great that may be. Such a philosophy, however, would be mistaken, because it would make the human will dependent on a factor (the surplus of pleasure over pain) which, at first, is wholly foreign to man's point of view. The original measure of his will is his desire, and desire asserts itself as long as it can. If I am compelled, in purchasing a certain quantity of apples, to take twice as many rotten ones as sound ones—because the seller wishes to clear out his stock—I shall not hesitate a moment to take the bad apples as well, if I put so high a value on the smaller quantity of good apples that I am prepared, in addition to the purchase price, to bear also the expense for the transportation of the rotten goods. This example illustrates the relation between the quantities of pleasure and of pain which are caused by a given instinct. I determine the value of the good apples, not by subtracting the sum of the good from that of the bad ones, but by the fact that, in spite of the presence of the bad ones, I still attach a value to the good ones.

Just as I leave out of account the bad apples in the enjoyment of the good ones, so I surrender myself to the satisfaction of a desire after having shaken off the inevitable pains.

Supposing even Pessimism were in the right with its assertion that the world contains more pain than pleasure, it would nevertheless have no influence upon the will, for living beings would still strive after such pleasure as remains. The empirical proof that pain overbalances pleasure is indeed effective for showing up the futility of that school of philosophy, which looks for the value of life in a surplus of pleasure (Eudæmonism), but not for exhibiting the will, as such, as irrational. For the will is not set upon a surplus of pleasure, but on whatever quantity of pleasure remains after subtracting the pain. This remaining pleasure still appears always as an object worth pursuing.

An attempt has been made to refute Pessimism by asserting that it is impossible to determine by calculation the surplus of pleasure or of pain in the world. The possibility of every calculation depends on our being able to compare the things to be calculated in respect of their quantity. Every pain and every pleasure has a definite quantity (intensity and duration). Further, we can compare pleasurable feelings of different kinds one with another, at least approximately, with regard to their intensity. We know whether we derive more pleasure from a good cigar or from a good joke. No objection can be raised against the comparability of different pleasures and pains in respect of their intensity. The thinker who sets himself the task of determining the surplus of pleasure or pain in the world, starts from presuppositions which are undeniably legitimate. It is possible to maintain that the Pessimistic results are false, but it is not possible to doubt that quantities of pleasure and pain can be scientifically estimated, and that the surplus of the one or the other can thereby be determined. It is incorrect, however, to assert that from this calculation any conclusions can be drawn for the human will. The cases in which we really make the value of our activity dependent on whether pleasure or pain shows a surplus, are those in which the objects towards which our activity is directed are indifferent to us. If it is a question whether, after the day's work, I am to amuse myself by a game or by light conversation, and if I am totally indifferent what I do so long as it amuses me, then I simply ask myself: What gives me the greatest surplus of pleasure? And I abandon the activity altogether if the scales incline towards the side of displeasure. If we are buying a toy for a child we consider, in selecting, what will give him the greatest pleasure, but in all other cases we are not determined exclusively by considerations of the balance of pleasure.

Hence, if Pessimistic thinkers believe that they are preparing the ground for an unselfish devotion to the work of civilisation, by demonstrating that there is a greater quantity of pain than of pleasure in life, they forget altogether that the human will is so constituted that it cannot be influenced by this knowledge. The whole striving of men is directed towards the greatest possible satisfaction that is attainable after overcoming all difficulties. The hope of this satisfaction is the basis of all human activity. The work of every single individual and the whole achievement of civilisation have their roots in this hope. The Pessimistic theory of Ethics thinks it necessary to represent the pursuit of pleasure as impossible, in order that man may devote himself to his proper moral tasks. But these moral tasks are nothing but the concrete natural and spiritual instincts; and he strives to satisfy these notwithstanding all incidental pain. The pursuit of pleasure, then, which the Pessimist sets himself to eradicate is nowhere to be found. But the tasks which man has to fulfil are fulfilled by him because from his very nature he wills to fulfil them. The Pessimistic system of Ethics maintains that a man cannot devote himself to what he recognises as his task in life until he has first given up the desire for pleasure. But no system of Ethics can ever invent other tasks than the realisation of those satisfactions which human desires demand, and the fulfilment of man's moral ideas. No Ethical theory can deprive him of the pleasure which he experiences in the realisation of what he desires. When the Pessimist says, "Do not strive after pleasure, for pleasure is unattainable; strive instead after what you recognise to be your task," we must reply that it is human nature to strive to do one's tasks, and that philosophy has gone astray in inventing the principle that man strives for nothing but pleasure. He aims at the satisfaction of what his nature demands, and the attainment of this satisfaction is to him a pleasure. Pessimistic Ethics, in demanding that we should strive, not after pleasure, but after the realisation of what we recognise as our task, lays its finger on the very thing which man wills in virtue of his own nature. There is no need for man to be turned inside out by philosophy, there is no need for him to discard his nature, in order to be moral. Morality means striving for an end so long as the pain connected with this striving does not inhibit the desire for the end altogether; and this is the essence of all genuine will. Ethics is not founded on the eradication of all desire for pleasure, in order that, in its place, bloodless moral ideas may set up their rule where no strong desire for pleasure stands in their way, but it is based on the strong will, sustained by ideal intuitions, which attains its end even when the path to it is full of thorns.

Moral ideals have their root in the moral imagination of man. Their realisation depends on the desire for them being sufficiently intense to overcome pains and agonies. They are man's own intuitions. In them his spirit braces itself to action. They are what he wills, because their realisation is his highest pleasure. He needs no Ethical theory first to forbid him to strive for pleasure and then to prescribe to him what he shall strive for. He will, of himself, strive for moral ideals provided his moral imagination is sufficiently active to inspire him with the intuitions, which give strength to his will to overcome all resistance.

If a man strives towards sublimely great ideals, it is because they are the content of his will, and because their realisation will bring him an enjoyment compared with which the pleasure which inferior spirits draw from the satisfaction of their commonplace needs is a mere nothing. Idealists delight in translating their ideals into reality.

Anyone who wants to eradicate the pleasure which the fulfilment of human desires brings, will have first to degrade man to the position of a slave who does not act because he wills, but because he must. For the attainment of the object of will gives pleasure. What we call the good is not what a man must do, but what he wills to do when he unfolds the fulness of his nature. Anyone who does not acknowledge this must deprive man of all the objects of his will, and then prescribe to him from without what he is to make the content of his will.

Man values the satisfaction of a desire because the desire springs from his own nature. What he attains is valuable because it is the object of his will. If we deny any value to the ends which men do will, then we shall have to look for the ends that are valuable among objects which men do not will.

A system of Ethics, then, which is built up on Pessimism has its root in the contempt for man's moral imagination. Only he who does not consider the individual human mind capable of determining for itself the content of its striving, can look for the sum and substance of will in the craving for pleasure. A man without imagination does not create moral ideas; they must be imparted to him. Physical nature sees to it that he seeks the satisfaction of his lower desires; but for the development of the whole man the desires which have their origin in the spirit are fully as necessary. Only those who believe that man has no such spiritual desires at all can maintain that they must be imparted to him from without. On that view it will also be correct to say that it is man's duty to do what he does not will to do. Every Ethical system which demands of man that he should suppress his will in order to fulfil tasks which he does not will, works, not with the whole man, but with a stunted being who lacks the faculty of spiritual desires. For a man who has been harmoniously developed, the so-called ideas of the Good lie, not without, but within the range of his will. Moral action consists, not in the extirpation of one's individual will, but in the fullest development of human nature. To regard moral ideals as attainable only on condition that man destroys his individual will, is to ignore the fact that these ideals are as much rooted in man's will as the satisfaction of the so-called animal instincts.

It cannot be denied that the views here outlined may easily be misunderstood. Immature youths without any moral imagination like to look upon the instincts of their half-developed natures as the full substance of humanity, and reject all moral ideas which they have not themselves originated, in order that they may "live themselves out" without restriction. But it goes without saying that a theory which holds for a fully developed man does not hold for half-developed boys. Anyone who still requires to be brought by education to the point where his moral nature breaks through the shell of his lower passions, cannot expect to be measured by the same standard as a mature man. But it was not my intention to set down what a half-fledged youth requires to be taught, but the essential nature of a mature man. My intention was to demonstrate the possibility of freedom, which becomes manifest, not in actions physically or psychically determined, but in actions sustained; by spiritual intuitions.

Every mature man is the maker of his own value. He does not aim at pleasure, which comes to him as a gift of grace on the part of Nature or of the Creator; nor does he live for the sake of what he recognises as duty, after he has put away from him the desire for pleasure. He acts as he wills, that is, in accordance with his moral intuitions; and he finds in the attainment of what he wills the true enjoyment of life. He determines the value of his life by measuring his attainments against his aims. An Ethical system which puts "ought" in the place of "will," duty in the place of inclination, is consistent in determining the value of man by the ratio between the demands of duty and his actual achievements. It applies to man a measure that is external to his own nature. The view which I have here developed points man back to himself. It recognises as the true value of life nothing except what each individual regards as such by the measure of his own will. A value of life which the individual does not recognise is as little acknowledged by my views as a purpose of life which does not spring from the value thus recognised. My view looks upon the individual as his own master and the assessor of his own value.

ADDITION TO THE REVISED EDITION (1918).

The argument of this chapter is open to misapprehension by those who obstinately insist on the apparent objection, that the will, as such, is the irrational factor in man, and that its irrationality should be exhibited in order to make man see, that the goal of his moral endeavour ought to be his ultimate emancipation from will. Precisely such an illusory objection has been brought against me by a competent critic who urged that it is the business of the philosopher to make good what animals and most men thoughtlessly forget, viz., to strike a genuine balance of life's account. But the objection ignores precisely the main point. If freedom is to be realised, the will in human nature must be sustained by intuitive thinking. At the same time we find that the will may also be determined by factors other than intuition, and that morality and its work can have no other root than the free realisation of intuition issuing from man's essential nature. Ethical Individualism is well fitted to exhibit morality in its full dignity. It does not regard true morality as the outward conformity of the will to a norm. Morality, for it, consists in the actions which issue from the unfolding of man's moral will as an integral part of his whole nature, so that immorality appears to man as a stunting and crippling of his nature.

1

Those who want to settle by calculation whether the sum total of pleasure or that of pain is bigger, ignore that they are subjecting to calculation something which is nowhere experienced. Feeling does not calculate, and what matters for the real valuing of life is what we really experience, not what results from an imaginary calculation.

2

We disregard here the case where excessive increase of pleasure turns pleasure into pain.

XIV

THE INDIVIDUAL AND THE GENUS

The view that man is a wholly self-contained, free individuality stands in apparent conflict with the facts, that he appears as a member of a natural whole (race, tribe, nation, family, male or female sex), and that he acts within a whole (state, church, etc.). He exhibits the general characteristics of the community to which he belongs, and gives to his actions a content which is defined by the place which he occupies within a social whole.

This being so, is any individuality left at all? Can we regard man as a whole in himself, in view of the fact that he grows out of a whole and fits as a member into a whole?

The character and function of a member of a whole are defined by the whole. A tribe is a whole, and all members of the tribe exhibit the peculiar characteristics which are conditioned by the nature of the tribe. The character and activity of the individual member are determined by the character of the tribe. Hence the physiognomy and the conduct of the individual have something generic about them. When we ask why this or that in a man is so or so, we are referred from the individual to the genus. The genus explains why something in the individual appears in the form observed by us.

But man emancipates himself from these generic characteristics. He develops qualities and activities the reason for which we can seek only in himself. The generic factors serve him only as a means to develop his own individual nature. He uses the peculiarities with which nature has endowed him as material, and gives them a form which expresses his own individuality. We seek in vain for the reason of such an expression of a man's individuality in the laws of the genus. We are dealing here with an individual who can be explained only through himself. If a man has reached the point of emancipation from what is generic in him, and we still attempt to explain all his qualities by reference to the character of the genus, then we lack the organ for apprehending what is individual.

It is impossible to understand a human being completely if one makes the concept of the genus the basis of one's judgment. The tendency to judge according to the genus is most persistent where differences of sex are involved. Man sees in woman, woman in man, almost always too much of the generic characteristics of the other's sex, and too little of what is individual in the other. In practical life this does less harm to men than to women. The social position of women is, in most instances, so low because it is not determined by the individual characteristics of each woman herself, but by the general ideas which are current concerning the natural function and needs of woman. A man's activity in life is determined by his individual capacity and inclination, whereas a woman's activity is supposed to be determined solely by the fact that she is just a woman. Woman is to be the slave of the generic, of the general idea of womanhood. So long as men debate whether woman, from her "natural disposition," is fitted for this, that, or the other profession, the so-called Woman's Question will never advance beyond the most elementary stage. What it lies in woman's nature to strive for had better be left to woman herself to decide. If it is true that women are fitted only for that profession which is theirs at present, then they will hardly have it in them to attain any other. But they must be allowed to decide for themselves what is conformable to their nature. To all who fear an upheaval of our social structure, should women be treated as individuals and not as specimens of their sex, we need only reply that a social structure in which the status of one-half of humanity is unworthy of a human being stands itself in great need of improvement.[1]

Anyone who judges human beings according to their generic character stops short at the very point beyond which they begin to be individuals whose activity rests on free self-determination. Whatever lies short of this point may naturally become matter for scientific study. Thus the characteristics of race, tribe, nation, and sex are the subject-matter of special sciences. Only men who are simply specimens of the genus could possibly fit the generic picture which the methods of these sciences produce. But all these sciences are unable to get as far as the unique character of the single individual. Where the sphere of freedom (thinking and acting) begins, there the possibility of determining the individual according to the laws of his genus ceases. The conceptual content which man, by an act of thought, has to connect with percepts, in order to possess himself fully of reality (*cp.* pp. 83 ff.), cannot be fixed by anyone once and for all, and handed down to humanity ready-made. The individual must gain his concepts through his own intuition. It is impossible to deduce from any concept of the genus how the individual ought to think; that depends singly and solely on the individual himself. So, again, it is just as impossible to determine, on the basis of the universal characteristics of human nature, what concrete ends the individual will set before himself. Anyone who wants to understand the single individual must penetrate to the innermost core of his being, and not stop short at those qualities which he shares with others. In this sense every single human being is a problem. And every science which deals only with abstract thoughts and generic concepts is but a preparation for the kind of knowledge which we gain when a human individual communicates to us his way of viewing the world, and for that other kind of knowledge which each of us gains from the content of his own will. Wherever we feel that here we are dealing with a man who has emancipated his thinking from all that is generic, and his will from the grooves typical of his kind, there we must cease to call in any concepts of our own making if we would understand his nature. Knowledge consists in the combination by thought of a concept and a percept. With all other objects the observer has to gain his concepts through his intuition. But if the problem is to understand a free individuality, we need only to take over into our own minds those concepts by which the individual determines himself, in their pure form (without admixture). Those who always mix their own ideas into their judgment on another person can never attain to the understanding of an individuality. Just as the free individual emancipates himself from the characteristics of the genus, so our knowledge of the individual must emancipate itself from the methods by which we understand what is generic.

A man counts as a free spirit in a human community only to the degree in which he has emancipated himself, in the way we have indicated, from all that is generic. No man is all genus, none is all individuality; but every man gradually emancipates a greater or lesser sphere of his being, both from the generic characteristics of animal life, and from the laws of human authorities which rule him despotically.

In respect of that part of his nature for which man is not able to win this freedom for himself, he forms a member within the organism of nature and of spirit. He lives, in this respect, by the imitation of others, or in obedience to their command. But ethical value belongs only to that part of his conduct which springs from his intuitions. And whatever moral instincts man possesses through the inheritance of social instincts, acquire ethical value through being taken up into his intuitions. In such ethical intuitions all moral activity of men has its root. To put this differently: the moral life of humanity is the sum-total of the products of the moral imagination of free human individuals. This is Monism's confession of faith.

1

Immediately upon the publication of this book (1894), critics objected to the above arguments that, even now, within the generic character of her sex, a woman is able to shape her life individually, just as she pleases, and far more freely than a man who is already de-individualised, first by the school, and later by war and profession. I am aware that this objection will be urged to-day, even more strongly. None the less, I feel bound to let my sentences stand, in the hope that there are readers who appreciate how violently such an objection runs counter to the concept of freedom advocated in this book, and who will interpret my sentences above by another standard than that of man's loss of individuality through school and profession.

ULTIMATE QUESTIONS

XV

THE CONSEQUENCES OF MONISM

An explanation of Nature on a single principle, or, in other words, Monism, derives from human experience all the material which it requires for the explanation of the world. In the same way, it looks for the springs of action also within the world of observation, *i.e.*, in that human part of Nature which is accessible to our self-observation, and more particularly in the moral imagination. Monism declines to seek outside that world the ultimate grounds of the world which we perceive and think. For Monism, the unity which reflective observation adds to the manifold multiplicity of percepts, is identical with the unity which the human desire for knowledge demands, and through which this desire seeks entrance into the physical and spiritual realms. Whoever looks for another unity behind this one, only shows that he fails to perceive the coincidence of the results of thinking with the demands of the instinct for knowledge. A particular human individual is not something cut off from the universe. He is a part of the universe, and his connection with the cosmic whole is broken, not in reality, but only for our perception. At first we apprehend the human part of the universe as a self-existing thing, because we are unable to perceive the cords and ropes by which the fundamental forces of the cosmos keep turning the wheel of our life.

All who remain at this perceptual standpoint see the part of the whole as if it were a truly independent, self-existing thing, a monad which gains all its knowledge of the rest of the world in some mysterious manner from without. But Monism has shown that we can believe in this independence only so long as thought does not gather our percepts into the network of the conceptual world. As soon as this happens, all partial existence in the universe, all isolated being, reveals itself as a mere appearance due to perception. Existence as a self-contained totality can be predicated only of the universe as a whole. Thought destroys the appearances due to perception and assigns to our individual existence a place in the life of the cosmos. The unity of the conceptual world which contains all objective percepts, has room also within itself for the content of our subjective personality. Thought gives us the true structure of reality as a self-contained unity, whereas the multiplicity of percepts is but an appearance conditioned by our organisation (*cp.* pp. 178 ff.). The recognition of the true unity of reality, as against the appearance of multiplicity, is at all times the goal of human thought. Science strives to apprehend our apparently disconnected percepts as a unity by tracing their inter-relations according to natural law. But, owing to the prejudice that an inter-relation discovered by human thought has only a subjective validity, thinkers have sought the true ground of unity in some object transcending the world of our experience (God, will, absolute spirit, etc.). Further, basing themselves on this prejudice, men have tried to gain, in addition to their knowledge of inter-relations within experience, a second kind of knowledge transcending experience, which should reveal the connection between empirical inter-relations and those realities which lie beyond the limits of experience (Metaphysics). The reason why, by logical thinking, we understand the nexus of the world, was thought to be that an original creator has built up the world according to logical laws, and, similarly, the ground of our actions was thought to lie in the will of this original being. It was overlooked that thinking embraces in one grasp the subjective and the objective, and that it communicates to us the whole of reality in the union which it effects between percept and concept. Only so long as we contemplate the laws which pervade and determine all percepts, in the abstract form of concepts, do we indeed deal only with something purely subjective. But this subjectivity does not belong to the content of the concept which, by means of thought, is added to the percept. This content is taken, not from the subject, but from reality. It is that part of reality which is inaccessible to perception. It is experience, but not the kind of experience which comes from perception. Those who cannot understand that the concept is something real, have in mind only the abstract form, in which we fix and isolate the concept. But in this isolation, the concept is as much dependent solely on our organisation as is the percept. The tree which I perceive, taken in isolation by itself, has no existence; it exists only as a member in the immense mechanism of Nature, and is possible only in real connection with Nature. An abstract concept, taken by itself, has as little reality as a percept taken by itself. The percept is that part of reality which is given objectively, the concept that part which is given subjectively (by intuition; *cp.* pp. 90 ff.). Our mental organisation breaks up reality into these two factors. The one factor is apprehended by perception, the other by intuition. Only the union of the two, which consists of the percept fitted according to law into its place in the universe, is reality in its full character. If we take mere percepts by themselves, we have no reality but only a disconnected chaos. If we take the laws which determine percepts by themselves, we have nothing but abstract concepts. Reality is not to be found in the abstract concept. It is revealed to the contemplative act of thought which regards neither the concept by itself nor the percept by itself, but the union of both.

Even the most orthodox Idealist will not deny that we live in the real world (that, as real beings, we are rooted in it); but he will deny that our knowledge, by means of its ideas, is able to grasp reality as we live it. As against this view, Monism shows that thought is neither subjective nor objective, but a principle which holds together both these sides of reality. The contemplative act of thought is a cognitive process which belongs itself to the sequence of real events. By thought we overcome, within the limits of experience itself, the one-sidedness of mere perception. We are not able by means of abstract conceptual hypotheses (purely conceptual speculation) to puzzle out the nature of the real, but in so far as we find for our percepts the right concepts we live in the real. Monism does not seek to supplement experience by something unknowable (transcending experience), but finds reality in concept and percept. It does not manufacture a metaphysical system out of pure concepts, because it looks upon concepts as only one side of reality, viz., the side which remains hidden from perception, but is meaningless except in union with percepts. But Monism gives man the conviction that he lives in the world of reality, and has no need to seek beyond the world for a higher reality. It refuses to look for Absolute Reality anywhere but in experience, because it recognises reality in the very content of experience. Monism is satisfied with this reality, because it knows that our thought points to no other. What Dualism seeks beyond the world of experience, that Monism finds in this world itself. Monism shows that our knowledge grasps reality in its true nature, not in a purely subjective image. It holds the conceptual content of the world to be identical for all human individuals (*cp.* pp. 84 ff.). According to Monistic principles, every human individual regards every other as akin to himself, because it is the same world-content which expresses itself in all. In the single conceptual world there are not as many concepts of "lion" as there are individuals who form the thought of "lion," but only one. And the concept which A adds to the percept of "lion" is identical with B's concept except so far as, in each case, it is apprehended by a different perceiving subject (*cp.* p. 85). Thought leads all perceiving subjects back to the ideal unity in all multiplicity, which is common to them all. There is but one ideal world, but it realises itself in human subjects as in a multiplicity of individuals. So long as man apprehends himself merely by self-observation, he looks upon himself as this particular being, but so soon as he becomes conscious of the ideal world which shines forth within him, and which embraces all particulars within itself, he perceives that the Absolute Reality lives within him. Dualism fixes upon the Divine Being as that which permeates all men and lives in them all. Monism finds this universal Divine Life in Reality itself. The ideal content of another subject is also my content, and I regard it as a different content only so long as I perceive, but no longer when I think. Every man embraces in his thought only a part of the total world of ideas, and so far, individuals are distinguished one from another also by the actual contents of their thought. But all these contents belong to a self-contained whole, which comprises within itself the thought-contents of all men. Hence every man, in so far as he thinks, lays hold of the universal Reality which pervades all men. To fill one's life with such thought-content is to live in Reality, and at the same time to live in God. The thought of a Beyond owes its origin to the misconception of those who believe that this world cannot have the ground of its existence in itself. They do not understand that, by thinking, they discover just what they demand for the explanation of the perceptual world. This is the reason why no speculation has ever produced any content which has not been borrowed from reality as it is given to us. A personal God is nothing but a human being transplanted into the Beyond. Schopenhauer's Will is the human will made absolute. Hartmann's Unconscious, made up of idea and will, is but a compound of two abstractions drawn from experience. Exactly the same is true of all other transcendent principles.

The truth is that the human mind never transcends the reality in which it lives. Indeed, it has no need to transcend it, seeing that this world contains everything that is required for its own explanation. If philosophers declare themselves finally content when they have deduced the world from principles which they borrow from experience and then transplant into an hypothetical Beyond, the same satisfaction ought to be possible, if these same principles are allowed to remain in this world to which they belong anyhow. All attempts to transcend the world are purely illusory, and the principles transplanted into the Beyond do not explain the world any better than the principles which are immanent in it. When thought understands itself, it does not demand any such transcendence at all, for there is no thought-content which does not find within the world a perceptual content, in union with which it can form a real object. The objects of imagination, too, are contents which have no validity, until they have been transformed into ideas that refer to a perceptual content. Through this perceptual content they have their place in reality. A concept the content of which is supposed to lie beyond the world which is given to us, is an abstraction to which no reality corresponds. Thought can discover only the concepts of reality; in order to find reality itself, we need also perception. An Absolute Being for which we invent a content, is a hypothesis which no thought can entertain that understands itself. Monism does not deny ideal factors; indeed, it refuses to recognise as fully real a perceptual content which has no ideal counterpart, but it finds nothing within the whole range of thought that is not immanent within this world of ours. A science which restricts itself to a description of percepts, without advancing to their ideal complements, is, for Monism, but a fragment. But Monism regards as equally fragmentary all abstract concepts which do not find their complement in percepts, and which fit nowhere into the conceptual net that embraces the whole perceptual world. Hence it knows no ideas referring to objects lying beyond our experience and supposed to form the content of purely hypothetical Metaphysics. Whatever mankind has produced in the way of such ideas Monism regards as abstractions from experience, whose origin in experience has been overlooked by their authors.

Just as little, according to Monistic principles, are the ends of our actions capable of being derived from the Beyond. So far as we can think them, they must have their origin in human intuition. Man does not adopt the purposes of an objective (transcendent) being as his own individual purposes, but he pursues the ends which his own moral imagination sets before him. The idea which realises itself in an action is selected by the agent from the single ideal world and made the basis of his will. Consequently his action is not a realisation of commands which have been thrust into this world from the Beyond, but of human intuitions which belong to this world. For Monism there is no ruler of the world standing outside of us and determining the aim and direction of our actions. There is for man no transcendent ground of existence, the counsels of which he might discover, in order thence to learn the ends to which he ought to direct his action. Man must rest wholly upon himself. He must himself give a content to his action. It is in vain that he seeks outside the world in which he lives for motives of his will. If he is to go at all beyond the satisfaction of the natural instincts for which Mother Nature has provided, he must look for motives in his own moral imagination, unless he finds it more convenient to let them be determined for him by the moral imagination of others. In other words, he must either cease acting altogether, or else act from motives which he selects for himself from the world of his ideas, or which others select for him from that same world. If he develops at all beyond a life absorbed in sensuous instincts and in the execution of the commands of others, then there is nothing that can determine him except himself. He has to act from a motive which he gives to himself and which nothing else can determine for him except himself. It is true that this motive is ideally determined in the single world of ideas; but in actual fact it must be selected by the agent from that world and translated into reality. Monism can find the ground for the actual realisation of an idea through human action only in the human being himself. That an idea should pass into action must be willed by man before it can happen. Such a will consequently has its ground only in man himself. Man, on this view, is the ultimate determinant of his action. He is free.

1. Addition to the Revised Edition (1918).

In the second part of this book the attempt has been made to justify the conviction that freedom is to be found in human conduct as it really is. For this purpose it was necessary to sort out, from the whole sphere of human conduct, those actions with respect to which unprejudiced self-observation may appropriately speak of freedom. These are the actions which appear as realisations of ideal intuitions. No other actions will be called free by an unprejudiced observer. However, open-minded self-observation compels man to regard himself as endowed with the capacity for progress on the road towards ethical intuitions and their realisation. Yet this open-minded observation of the ethical nature of man is, by itself, insufficient to constitute the final court of appeal for the question of freedom. For, suppose intuitive thinking had itself sprung from some other essence; suppose its essence were not grounded in itself, then the consciousness of freedom, which issues from moral conduct, would prove to be a mere illusion. But the second part of this book finds its natural support in the first part, which presents intuitive thinking as an inward spiritual activity which man experiences as such. To appreciate through experience this essence of thinking is equivalent to recognising the freedom of intuitive thinking. And once we know that this thinking is free, we know also the sphere within which will may be called free. We shall regard man as a free agent, if on the basis of inner experience we may attribute to the life of intuitive thinking a self-sustaining essence. Whoever cannot do this will be unable to discover any wholly unassailable road to the belief in freedom. The experience to which we here refer reveals in consciousness intuitive thinking, the reality of which does not depend merely on our being conscious of it. Freedom, too, is thereby revealed as the characteristic of all actions which issue from the intuitions of consciousness.

2. Addition to the Revised Edition (1918).

The argumentation of this book is built up on the fact of intuitive thinking, which may be experienced in a purely spiritual way, and which every perception inserts into reality so that reality comes thereby to be known. All that this book aimed at presenting was the result of a survey from the basis of our experience of intuitive thinking. However, the intention also was to emphasise the systematic interpretation which this thinking, as experienced by us, demands. It demands that we shall not deny its presence in cognition as a self-sustaining experience. It demands that we acknowledge its capacity for experiencing reality in co-operation with perception, and that we do not make it seek reality in a world outside experience and accessible only to inference, in the face of which human thinking would be only a subjective activity.

This view characterises thinking as that factor in man through which he inserts himself spiritually into reality. (And, strictly, no one should confuse this kind of world-view, which is based on thinking as directly experienced, with mere Rationalism.) But, on the other hand, the whole tenor of the preceding argumentation shows that perception yields a determination of reality for human knowledge only when it is taken hold of in thinking. Outside of thinking there is nothing to characterise reality for what it is. Hence we have no right to imagine that sense-perception is the only witness to reality. Whatever comes to us by way of perception on our journey through life, we cannot but expect. The only point open to question would be whether, from the exclusive point of view of thinking as we intuitively experience it, we have a right to expect that over and above sensuous perception there is also spiritual perception. This expectation is justified. For, though intuitive thinking is, on the one hand, an active process taking place in the human mind, it is, on the other hand, also a spiritual perception mediated by no sense-organ. It is a perception in which the percipient is himself active, and a self-activity which is at the same time perceived. In intuitive thinking man enters a spiritual world also as a percipient. Whatever within this world presents itself to him as percept in the same way in which the spiritual world of his own thinking so presents itself, that is recognised by him as constituting a world of spiritual perception. This world of spiritual perception we may suppose to be standing in the same relation to thinking as does, on the sensuous side, the world of sense-perception. Man does not experience the world of spiritual perception as an alien something, because he is already familiar in his intuitive thinking with an experience of purely spiritual character. With such a world of spiritual perception a number of the writings are concerned which I have published since this present book appeared. The *Philosophy of Spiritual Activity* lays the philosophical foundation for these later writings. For it attempts to show that in the very experience of thinking, rightly understood, we experience Spirit. This is the reason why it appears to the author that no one will stop short of entering the world of spiritual perception who has been able to adopt, in all seriousness, the point of view of the *Philosophy of Spiritual Activity*. True, logical deduction—by syllogisms—will not extract out of the contents of this book the contents of the author's later books. But a living understanding of what is meant in this book by "intuitive thinking" will naturally prepare the way for living entry into the world of spiritual perception.

TRUTH AND SCIENCE

I

PRELIMINARY OBSERVATIONS

Theory of Knowledge aims at being a scientific investigation of the very fact which all other sciences take for granted without examination, viz., knowing or knowledge-getting itself. To say this is to attribute to it, from the very start, the character of being the fundamental philosophical discipline. For, it is only this discipline which can tell us what value and significance belong to the insight gained by the other sciences. In this respect it is the foundation for all scientific endeavour. But, it is clear that the Theory of Knowledge can fulfil its task only if it works without any presuppositions of its own, so far as that is possible in view of the nature of human knowledge. This is probably conceded on all sides. And yet, a more detailed examination of the better-known epistemological systems reveals that, at the very starting-point of the inquiry, there is made a whole series of assumptions which detract considerably from the plausibility of the rest of the argument. In particular, it is noticeable how frequently certain hidden assumptions are made in the very formulation of the fundamental problems of epistemology. But, if a science begins by misstating its problems, we must despair from the start of finding the right solution. The history of the sciences teaches us that countless errors, from which whole epochs have suffered, are to be traced wholly and solely to the fact that certain problems were wrongly formulated. For illustrations there is no need to go back to Aristotle or to the Ars Magna Lulliana. There are plenty of examples in more recent times. The numerous questions concerning the purposes of the rudimentary organs of certain organisms could be correctly formulated only after the discovery of the fundamental law of biogenesis had created the necessary conditions. As long as Biology was under the influence of teleological concepts, it was impossible to put these problems in a form permitting a satisfactory answer. What fantastic ideas, for example, were current concerning the purpose of the so-called pineal gland, so long as it was fashionable to frame biological questions in terms of "purpose." An answer was not achieved until the solution of the problem was sought by the method of Comparative Anatomy, and scientists asked whether this organ might not be merely a residual survival in man from a lower evolutionary level. Or, to mention yet another example, consider the modifications in certain physical problems after the discovery of the laws of the mechanical equivalents of heat and of the conservation of energy! In short, the success of scientific investigations depends essentially upon the investigator's ability to formulate his problems correctly. Even though the Theory of Knowledge, as the presupposition of all other sciences, occupies a position very different from theirs, we may yet expect that for it, too, successful progress in its investigations will become possible only when the fundamental questions have been put in the correct form.

The following discussions aim, in the first place, at such a formulation of the problem of knowledge as will do justice to the character of the Theory of Knowledge as a discipline which is without any presuppositions whatever. Their secondary aim is to throw light on the relation of J. G. Fichte's *Wissenschaftslehre* to such a fundamental philosophical discipline. The reason why precisely Fichte's attempt to provide an absolutely certain basis for the sciences will be brought into closer relation with our own philosophical programme, will become clear of itself in the course of our investigation.

II

THE FUNDAMENTAL PROBLEM OF KANT'S THEORY OF KNOWLEDGE

It is usual to designate Kant as the founder of the Theory of Knowledge in the modern sense. Against this view it might plausibly be argued that the history of philosophy records prior to Kant numerous investigations which deserve to be regarded as something more than mere beginnings of such a science. Thus Volkelt, in his fundamental work on the Theory of Knowledge,[1] remarks that the critical treatment of this discipline took its origin already with Locke. But in the writings of even older philosophers, yes, even in the philosophy of Ancient Greece, discussions are to be found which at the present day are usually undertaken under the heading of Theory of Knowledge. However, Kant has revolutionised all problems under this head from their very depths up, and, following him, numerous thinkers have worked them through so thoroughly that all the older attempts at solutions may be found over again either in Kant himself or else in his successors. Hence, for the purposes of a purely systematic, as distinct from a historical, study of the Theory of Knowledge, there is not much danger of omitting any important phenomenon by taking account only of the period since Kant burst upon the world with his *Critique of Pure Reason*. All previous epistemological achievements are recapitulated during this period.

The fundamental question of Kant's Theory of Knowledge is, *How are synthetic judgments a priori possible?* Let us consider this question for a moment in respect of its freedom from presuppositions. Kant asks the question precisely because he believes that we can attain unconditionally certain knowledge only if we are able to prove the validity of synthetic judgments *a priori*. He says: "Should this question be answered in a satisfactory way, we shall at the same time learn what part reason plays in the foundation and completion of those sciences which contain a theoretical *a priori* knowledge of objects;"[2] and, further, "Metaphysics stands and falls with the solution of this problem, on which, therefore, the very existence of Metaphysics absolutely depends."[3]

Are there any presuppositions in this question, as formulated by Kant? Yes, there are. For the possibility of a system of absolutely certain knowledge is made dependent on its being built up exclusively out of judgments which are synthetic and acquired independently of all experience. "Synthetic" is Kant's term for judgments in which the concept of the predicate adds to the concept of the subject something which lies wholly outside the subject, "although it stands in some connection with the subject,"[4] whereas in "analytic" judgments the predicate affirms only what is already (implicitly) contained in the subject. This is not the place for considering the acute objections which Johannes Rehmke[5] brings forward against this classification of judgments. For our present purpose, it is enough to understand that we can attain to genuine knowledge only through judgments which add to one concept another the content of which was not, *for us* at least, contained in that of the former. If we choose to call this class of judgments, with Kant, "synthetic," we may agree that knowledge in judgment form is obtainable only where the connection of predicate and subject is of this synthetic sort. But, the case is very different with the second half of Kant's question, which demands that these judgments are to be formed *a priori, i.e.,* independently of all experience. For one thing, it is altogether possible[6] that such judgments do not occur at all. At the start of the Theory of Knowledge we must hold entirely open the question, whether we arrive at any judgments otherwise than by experience, or only by experience. Indeed, to unprejudiced reflection the alleged independence of experience seems from the first to be impossible. For, let the object of our knowledge be what it may—it must, surely, always present itself to us at some time in an immediate and unique way; in short, it must become for us an experience. Mathematical judgments, too, are known by us in no other way than by our experiencing them in particular concrete cases. Even if, with Otto Liebmann,[7] for example, we treat them as founded upon a certain organisation of our consciousness, this empirical character is none the less manifest. We shall then say that this or that proposition is necessarily valid, because the denial of its truth would imply the denial of our consciousness, but the content of a proposition can enter our knowledge only by its becoming an experience for us in exactly the same way in which a process in the outer world of nature does so. Let the content of such a proposition include factors which guarantee its absolute validity, or let its validity be based on other grounds—in either case, I can possess myself of it only in one way and in no other: it must be presented to me in experience. This is the first objection to Kant's view.

The other objection lies in this, that we have no right, at the outset of our epistemological investigations, to affirm that no absolutely certain knowledge can have its source in experience. Without doubt, it is easily conceivable that experience itself might contain a criterion guaranteeing the certainty of all knowledge which has an empirical source.

Thus, Kant's formulation of the problem implies two presuppositions. The first is that we need, over and above experience, another source of cognitions. The second is that all knowledge from experience has only conditional validity. Kant entirely fails to realise that these two propositions are open to doubt, that they stand in need of critical examination. He takes them over as unquestioned assumptions from the dogmatic philosophy of his predecessors and makes them the basis of his own critical inquiries. The dogmatic thinkers assume the validity of these two propositions and simply apply them in order to get from each the kind of knowledge which it guarantees. Kant assumed their validity and only asks, What are the conditions of their validity? But, what if they are not valid at all? In that case, the edifice of Kantian doctrine lacks all foundation whatever.

The whole argumentation of the five sections which precede Kant's formulation of the problem, amounts to an attempt to prove that the propositions of Mathematics are synthetic.[8] But, precisely the two presuppositions which we have pointed out are retained as mere assumptions in his discussions. In the Introduction to the Second Edition of the *Critique of Pure Reason* we read, "experience can tell us that a thing is so and so, but not that it cannot be otherwise," and, "experience never bestows on its judgments true or strict universality, but only the assumed and relative universality of induction."[9] In *Prologomena*,[10] we find it said,

"First, as regards the *sources* of metaphysics, the very concept of Metaphysics implies that they cannot be empirical. The principles of Metaphysics (where the term 'principles' includes, not merely its fundamental propositions, but also its fundamental concepts), can never be gained from experience, for the knowledge of the metaphysician has precisely to be, not physical, but 'metaphysical,' *i.e.*, lying beyond the reach of experience." Lastly Kant says in the *Critique of Pure Reason*: "The first thing to notice is, that no truly mathematical judgments are empirical, but always *a priori*. They carry necessity on their very face, and therefore cannot be derived from experience. Should anyone demur to this, I am willing to limit my assertion to the propositions of *Pure Mathematics*, which, as everybody will admit, are not empirical judgments, but perfectly pure *a priori* knowledge."[11]

We may open the *Critique of Pure Reason* wherever we please, we shall always find that in all its discussions these two dogmatic propositions are taken for granted. Cohen[12] and Stadler[13] attempt to prove that Kant has established the *a priori* character of the propositions of Mathematics and Pure Natural Science. But all that Kant tries to do in the *Critique* may be summed up as follows. The fact that Mathematics and Pure Natural Science are *a priori* sciences implies that the "form" of all experience has its ground in the subject. Hence, all that is given by experience is the "matter" of sensations. This matter is synthesised by the forms, inherent in the mind, into the system of empirical science. It is only as principles of order for the matter of sense that the formal principles of the *a priori* theories have function and significance. They make empirical science possible, but they cannot transcend it. These formal principles are nothing but the synthetic judgments *a priori*, which therefore extend, as conditions of all possible empirical knowledge, as far as that knowledge but no further. Thus, the *Critique of Pure Reason*, so far from proving the a *priori* character of Mathematics and Pure Natural Science, does but delimit the sphere of their applicability on the assumption that their principles must become known independently of experience. Indeed, Kant is so far from attempting a proof of the *a priori* character of these principles, that he simply excludes that part of Mathematics (see the quotation above) in which, even according to his view, that character might be called in question, and confines himself to the part in which he thinks he can infer the *a priori* character from the bare concepts involved. Johannes Volkelt, too, comes to the conclusion that "Kant starts from the explicit presupposition" that "there actually does exist knowledge which is universal and necessary." He goes on to remark, "This presupposition which Kant has never explicitly questioned, is so profoundly contradictory to the character of a truly critical Theory of Knowledge, that the question must be seriously put whether the *Critique* is to be accepted as critical Theory of Knowledge at all." Volkelt does, indeed, decide that there are good grounds for answering this question in the affirmative, but still, as he says, "this dogmatic assumption does disturb the critical attitude of Kant's epistemology in the most far-reaching way."[14] In short, Volkelt, too, finds that the *Critique of Pure Reason* is not a Theory of Knowledge free from all assumptions.

In substantial agreement with our view are also the views of O. Liebmann,[15] Holder,[16] Windelband,[17] Ueberweg,[18] Eduard von Hartmann,[19] and Kuno Fischer,[20] all of whom acknowledge that Kant makes the *a priori* character of Pure Mathematics and Physics the basis of his whole argumentation.

The propositions that we really have knowledge which is independent of all experience, and that experience can furnish knowledge of only relative universality, could be accepted by us as valid only if they were conclusions deduced from other propositions. It would be absolutely necessary for these propositions to be preceded by an inquiry into the essential nature of experience, as well as by another inquiry into the essential nature of knowing. The former might justify the first, the latter the second, of the above two propositions.

It would be possible to reply to the objections which we have urged against the *Critique of Pure Reason*, as follows. It might be said that every Theory of Knowledge must first lead the reader to the place where the starting-point, free from all presuppositions, is to be found. For, the knowledge which we have at any given moment of our lives is far removed from this starting-point, so that we must first be artificially led back to it. Now, it is true that some such mutual understanding between author and reader concerning the starting-point of the science is necessary in all Theory of Knowledge. But such an understanding ought on no account to go beyond showing how far the alleged starting-point of knowing is truly such. It ought to consist of purely self-evident, analytic propositions. It ought not to lay down any positive, substantial affirmations which influence, as in Kant, the content of the subsequent argumentation. Moreover, it is the duty of the epistemologist to show that the starting-point which he alleges is really free from all presuppositions. But all this has nothing to do with the essential nature of that starting-point. It lies wholly outside the starting-point and makes no affirmations about it. At the beginning of mathematical instruction, too, the teacher must exert himself to convince the pupil of the axiomatic character of certain principles. But no one will maintain that the *content* of the axioms is in any way made dependent on these prior discussions of their axiomatic character.[21] In exactly the same way, the epistemologist, in his introductory remarks, ought to show the method by which we can reach a starting-point free from all presuppositions. But the real content of the starting-point ought to be independent of the reflections by which it is discovered. There is, most certainly, a wide difference between such an introduction to the Theory of Knowledge and Kant's way of beginning with affirmations of quite definite, dogmatic character.

1

l.c., p. 20.

2

cf. Kant, *Critique of Pure Reason*, Intr. to 2nd edit., Section vi.

3

Prolegomena, Section v.

4

Critique of Pure Reason, Intr., Section iv.

5

cf. his *Analyse der Wirklichkeit, Gedanken und Tatsachen.*

6

"Possible" here means merely *conceivable.*

7

cf. Die Welt als Wahrnehmung und Begriff, pp. 161 ff.

8

This attempt, by the way, is one which the objections of Robert Zimmermann (*Über Kant's mathematisches Vorurteil und dessen Folgen*) show to be, if not wholly mistaken, at least highly questionable.

9

Critique of Pure Reason, Intr. to 2nd edit., Section ii.

10

cf. Kant's Theorie der Erfahrung, pp. 90 ff.

11

l.c., Section v.

12

cf. Kant's Theorie der Erfahrung, pp. 90 ff.

13

cf. Die Grundsätze der reinen Erkenntnistheorie in der Kantischen Philosophie, p. 76.

14

l.c., p. 21.

15

Zur Analyse der Wirklichkeit, pp. 211 ff.

16

Darstellung der Kantischen Erkenntnistheorie, p. 14.

17

Vierteljahrsschrift für Wissenschaftliche Philosophie, 1877, p. 239.

18

System der Logik, 3rd edit., pp. 380 ff.

19

Kritische Grundlagen des Transcendentalen Realismus, pp. 142–172.

20

Geschichte der Neueren Philosophie, Vol. v., p. 60. Volkelt is mistaken about Fischer when he says (*Kant's Erkenntnistheorie,* p. 198, *n.*) that "it is not clear from Fischer's account whether, in his opinion, Kant takes for granted only the psychological fact of the occurrence of universal and necessary judgments, but also their objective validity and truth." For, in the passage referred to above, Fischer says that the chief difficulty of the *Critique of Pure Reason* is to be found in the fact that "its fundamental positions rest on certain presuppositions" which "have to be granted if the rest is to be valid." These presuppositions consist for Fischer, too, in this, that "first the fact of knowledge is affirmed," and then analysis reveals the cognitive faculties "by means of which that fact itself is explained."

21

How far our own epistemological discussions conform to this method, will be shown in Section iv, "The Starting-points of the Theory of Knowledge."

III

THEORY OF KNOWLEDGE SINCE KANT

Kant's mistaken formulation of the problem has had a greater or lesser influence on all subsequent students of the Theory of Knowledge. For Kant, the view that all objects which are given to us in experience are *ideas* in our minds is a *consequence* of his theory of the *a priori*. For nearly all his successors, it has become the first principle and starting-point of their epistemological systems. It is said that the first and most immediate truth is, simply and solely, the proposition that we know our own ideas. This has come to be a well-nigh universal conviction among philosophers. G. E. Schulze maintains in his *Ænesidemus*, as early as 1792, that all our cognitions are mere ideas and that we can never transcend our ideas. Schopenhauer puts forward, with all the philosophical pathos which distinguishes him, the view that the permanent achievement of Kant's philosophy is the thesis that "the world is my idea." To Eduard von Hartmann this thesis is so incontestable, that he addresses his treatise, *Kritische Grundlegung des Transcendentalen Realismus*, exclusively to readers who have achieved critical emancipation from the naïve identification of the world of perception with the thing-in-itself. He demands of them that they shall have made clear to themselves the *absolute heterogeneity* of the object of perception which through the act of representation has been given as a subjective and ideal content of consciousness, and of the thing-in-itself which is independent of the act of representation and of the form of consciousness and which exists in its own right. His readers are required to be thoroughly convinced that the whole of what is immediately given to us consists of *ideas*.[1] In his latest work on Theory of Knowledge, Hartmann does, indeed, attempt to give reasons for this view. What value should be attached to these reasons by an unprejudiced Theory of Knowledge will appear in the further course of our discussions. Otto Liebmann posits as the sacrosanct first principle of the Theory of Knowledge the proposition, "Consciousness cannot transcend itself."[2] Volkelt has called the proposition that the first and most immediate truth is the limitation of all our knowledge, in the first instance, to our own ideas exclusively, the *positivistic principle of knowledge*. He regards only those theories of knowledge as "in the fullest sense critical" which "place this principle, as the only fixed starting-point of philosophy, at the head of their discussions and then consistently think out its consequences."[3] Other philosophers place other propositions at the head of the Theory of Knowledge, *e.g.*, the proposition that its real problem concerns the relation between Thought and Being, and the possibility of a mediation between them;[4] or that it concerns the way in which Being becomes an object of Consciousness;[5] and many others. Kirchmann starts from two epistemological axioms, "Whatever is perceived is," and, "Whatever is self-contradictory, is not."[6] According to E. L. Fischer, knowledge is the science of something *actual*, something *real*,[7] and he criticises this dogma as little as does Goering who asserts similarly, "To know means always to know something which is. This is a fact which cannot be denied either by scepticism or by Kant's critical philosophy."[8] These two latter thinkers simply lay down the law: This is what knowledge is. They do not trouble to ask themselves with what right they do it.

But, even if these various propositions were correct, or led to correct formulations of the problem, it would still be impossible to discuss them at the outset of the Theory of Knowledge. *For, they all belong, as positive and definite cognitions, within the realm of knowledge.* To say that my knowledge extends, in the first instance, only to my ideas, is to express in a perfectly definite judgment something which I *know*. In this judgment I qualify the world which is given to me by the predicate "existing in the form of idea." But how am I to know, *prior to all knowledge*, that the objects given to me are *ideas*?

The best way to convince ourselves of the truth of the assertion that this proposition has no right to be put at the head of the Theory of Knowledge, is to retrace the way which the human mind must follow in order to reach this proposition, which has become almost an integral part of the whole modern scientific consciousness. The considerations which have led to it are systematically summarised, with approximate exhaustiveness, in Part I of Eduard von Hartmann's treatise, *Das Grundproblem der Erkenntnistheorie*. His statement, there, may serve as a sort of guiding-thread for us in our task of reviewing the reasons which may lead to the acceptance of this proposition.

These reasons are physical, psycho-physical, physiological, and properly philosophical.

The Physicist is led by observation of the phenomena which occur in our environment when, *e.g.*, we experience a sensation of sound, to the view that there is nothing in these phenomena which in the very least resembles what we perceive immediately as sound. Outside, in the space which surrounds us, nothing is to be found except longitudinal oscillations of bodies and of the air. Thence it is inferred that what in ordinary life we call "sound" or "tone" is nothing but the subjective reaction of our organism to these wave-like oscillations. Similarly, it is inferred that light and colour and heat are purely subjective. The phenomena of colour-dispersion, of refraction, of interference, of polarisation, teach us that to the just-mentioned sensations there correspond in the outer space certain transverse oscillations which we feel compelled to ascribe, in part to the bodies, in part to an immeasurably fine, elastic fluid, the "ether." Further, the Physicist is driven by certain phenomena in the world of bodies to abandon the belief in the continuity of objects in space, and to analyse them into systems of exceedingly minute particles (molecules, atoms), the size of which, relatively to the distances between them, is immeasurably small. Thence it is inferred that all action of bodies on each other is across the empty intervening space, and is thus a genuine *actio in distans*. The Physicist believes himself justified in holding that the action of bodies on our senses of touch and temperature does not take place through direct contact, because there must always remain a definite, if small, distance between the body and the spot on the skin which it is said to "touch." Thence it is said to follow that what we sense as hardness or heat in bodies is nothing but the reactions of the end-organs of our touch- and temperature-nerves to the *molecular forces* of bodies which act upon them across empty space.

These considerations from the sphere of Physics are supplemented by the Psycho-physicists with their doctrine of specific sense-energies. J. Müller has shown that every sense can be affected only in its own characteristic way as determined by its organisation, and that its reaction is always of the same kind whatever may be the external stimulus. If the optical nerve is stimulated, light-sensations are experienced by us regardless of whether the stimulus was pressure, or an electric current, or light. On the other hand, the same external phenomena produce quite different sensations according as they are perceived by different senses. From these facts the inference has been drawn that there occurs only *one sort* of phenomenon in the external world, viz., motions, and that the variety of qualities of the world we perceive is essentially a reaction of our senses to these motions. According to this view, we do not perceive the external world as such, but only the subjective sensations which it evokes in us.

Physiology adds its quota to the physical arguments. Physics deals with the phenomena which occur outside our organisms and which correspond to our percepts. Physiology seeks to investigate the processes which go on in man's own body when a certain sensation is evoked in him. It teaches us that the epidermis is wholly insensitive to the stimuli in the external world. Thus, *e.g.*, if external stimuli are to affect the end-organs of our touch-nerves on the surface of our bodies, the oscillations which occur outside our bodies have to be transmitted through the epidermis. In the case of the senses of hearing and of sight, the external motions have, in addition, to be modified by a number of structures in the sense-organs, before they reach the nerves. The nerves have to conduct the effects produced in the end-organs up to the central organ, and only then can take place the process by means of which purely mechanical changes in the brain produce sensations. It is clear that the stimulus which acts upon the sense-organs is so completely changed by the transformations which it undergoes, that every trace of resemblance between the initial impression on the sense-organs and the final sensation in consciousness must be obliterated. Hartmann sums up the outcome of these considerations in these words: "This content of consciousness consists, originally, of sensations which are the reflex responses of the soul to the molecular motions in the highest cortical centres, but which have not the faintest resemblance to the molecular motions by which they are elicited."

If we think this line of argument through to the end, we must agree that, assuming it to be correct, there survives in the content of our consciousness not the least element of what may be called "external existence."

To the physical and physiological objections against so-called "Naïve Realism" Hartmann adds some further objections which he describes as philosophical in the strict sense. A logical examination of the physical and physiological objections reveals that, after all, the desired conclusion can be reached only if we start from the existence and nexus of external objects, just as these are assumed by the ordinary naïve consciousness, and then inquire how this external world can enter the consciousness of beings with organisms such as ours. We have seen that every trace of such an external world is lost on the way from the impression on the sense-organ to the appearance of the sensation in our consciousness, and that in the latter nothing survives except our ideas. Hence, we have to assume that the picture of the external world which we actually have, has been built up by the soul on the basis of the sensations given to it. First, the soul constructs out of the data of the senses of touch and sight a picture of the world in space, and then the sensations of the other senses are fitted into this space-system. When we are compelled to think of a certain complex of sensations as belonging together, we are led to the concept of substance and regard substance as the bearer of sense-qualities. When we observe that some sense-qualities disappear from a substance and that others appear in their place, we ascribe this event in the world of phenomena to a change regulated by the law of causality. Thus, according to this view, our whole world-picture is composed of subjective sensations which are ordered by the activity of our own souls. Hartmann says, "What the subject perceives is always only modifications of its own psychic states and nothing else."[9]

Now let us ask ourselves, How do we come by such a view? The bare skeleton of the line of thought which leads to it is as follows. Supposing an external world exists, we do not perceive it as such but transform it through our organisation into a world of ideas. This is a supposition which, when consistently thought out, destroys itself. But is this reflection capable of supporting any positive alternative? Are we justified in regarding the world, which is given to us, as the subjective content of ideas because the assumptions of the naïve consciousness, logically followed out, lead to this conclusion? Our purpose is, rather, to exhibit these assumptions themselves as untenable. Yet, so far we should have found only that it is possible for a premise to be false and yet for the conclusion drawn from it to be true. Granted that this may happen, yet we can never regard the conclusion as *proved* by means of that premise.

It is usual to apply the title of "Naïve Realism" to the theory which accepts as self-evident and indubitable the reality of the world-picture which is immediately given to us. The opposite theory, which regards this world as merely the content of our consciousness, is called "Transcendental Idealism." Hence, we may sum up the outcome of the above discussion by saying, "*Transcendental Idealism demonstrates its own truth, by employing the premises of the Naïve Realism which it seeks to refute.*" Transcendental Idealism is true, if Naïve Realism is false. But the falsity of the latter is shown only by assuming it to be true. Once we clearly realise this situation, we have no choice but to abandon this line of argument and to try another. But are we to trust to good luck, and experiment about until we hit by accident upon the right line? This is Eduard von Hartmann's view when he believes himself to have shown the validity of his own epistemological standpoint, on the ground that his theory explains the phenomena whereas its rivals do not. According to his view, the several philosophical systems are engaged in a sort of struggle for existence in which the fittest is ultimately accepted as victor. But this method appears to us to be unsuitable, if only for the reason that there may well be several hypotheses which explain the phenomena *equally* satisfactorily. Hence, we had better keep to the above line of thought for the refutation of Naïve Realism, and see where precisely its deficiency lies. For, after all, Naïve Realism is the view from which we all start out. For this reason alone it is advisable to begin by setting it right. When we have once understood why it must be defective, we shall be led upon the right path with far greater certainty than if we proceed simply at haphazard.

The subjectivism which we have sketched above is the result of the elaboration of certain facts by *thought*. Thus, it takes for granted that, from given facts as starting-point, we can by consistent thinking, *i.e.*, by logical combination of certain observations, gain correct conclusions. But our *right* thus to employ our thinking remains unexamined. There, precisely, lies the weakness of this method. Whereas Naïve Realism starts from the unexamined assumption that the contents of our perceptual experience have objective reality, the Idealism just described starts from the no less unexamined conviction that by the use of thought we can reach conclusions which are scientifically valid. In contrast to Naïve Realism, we may call this point of view "Naïve Rationalism." In order to justify this term, it may be well to insert here a brief comment on the concept of the "Naïve." A. Döring, in his essay *Über den Begriff des Naiven Realismus*,[10] attempts a more precise determination of this concept. He says, "The concept of the Naïve marks as it were the zero-point on the scale of our reflection upon our own activity. In content the Naïve may well coincide with the True, for, although the Naïve is unreflecting and, therefore, uncritical or a-critical, yet this lack of reflection and criticism excludes only the objective assurance of truth. It implies the possibility and the danger of error, but it does not imply the necessity of error. There are naïve modes of feeling and willing as there are naïve modes of apprehending and thinking, in the widest sense of the latter term. Further, there are naïve modes of expressing these inward states in contrast with their repression or modification through consideration for others and through reflection. Naïve activity is not influenced, at least not consciously, by tradition, education, or imposed rule. It is in all spheres (as its root *nativus*, brings out), unconscious, impulsive, instinctive, dæmonic activity." Starting from this account, we will try to determine the concept of the Naïve still more precisely. In every activity we may consider two aspects—the activity itself and our consciousness of its conformity to a law. We may be wholly absorbed in the former, without caring at all for the latter. The artist is in this position, who does not know in reflective form the laws of his creative activity but yet *practises* these laws by feeling and sense. We call him "naïve." But there is a kind of self-observation which inquires into the laws of one's own activity and which replaces the naïve attitude, just described, by the consciousness of knowing exactly the scope and justification of all one does. This we will call "critical." This account seems to us best to hit off the meaning of this concept which, more or less clearly understood, has since Kant acquired citizen-rights in the world of philosophy. Critical reflection is, thus, the opposite of naïve consciousness. We call an attitude "critical" which makes itself master of the laws of its own activity in order to know how far it can rely on them and what are their limits. Theory of Knowledge can be nothing if not a critical science. Its object is precisely the most subjective activity of man—knowing. What it aims at exhibiting is the laws to which knowing conforms. Hence, the naïve attitude is wholly excluded from this science. Its claim to strength lies precisely in that it achieves what many minds, interested in practice rather than in theory, pride themselves on never having attempted, viz., "thinking about thought."

1

l.c., Preface, p. x.

2

Zur Analyse der Wirklichkeit (Strassburg, 1876), p. 28.

3

Kant's Erkenntnistheorie, Section i.

4

A. Dorner, *Das menschliche Erkennen* (Berlin, 1887).

5

Rehmke, *l.c.*

6

Die Lehre vom Wissen (Berlin, 1868).

7

Die Grundfragen der Erkenntnistheorie (Mainz, 1887) p. 385.

8

System der kritischen Philosophie, I. Teil, p. 257.

9

Das Grundproblem der Erkenntnistheorie, p. 37.

Philosophische Monatshefte, Vol. xxvi (1890), p. 390.

IV

THE STARTING-POINTS OF THE THEORY OF KNOWLEDGE

At the beginning of an epistemological inquiry we must, in accordance with the conclusions we have reached, put aside everything which we have come to know. For, knowledge is something which man has produced, something which he has originated by his activity. If the Theory of Knowledge is really to extend the light of its explanation over the *whole* field of what we know, it must set out from a point which has remained wholly untouched by cognitive activity—indeed which rather furnishes the first impulse for this activity. The point at which we must start lies *outside* of what we know. It cannot as yet itself be an item of knowledge. But we must look for it *immediately prior* to the act of cognition, so that the very next step which man takes shall be a *cognitive* act. The method for determining this absolutely first starting-point must be such that nothing enters into it which is already the result of cognitive activity.

There is nothing but the *immediately-given* world-picture with which we can make a start of this sort. This means the picture of the world which is presented to man before he has in any way transformed it by cognitive activity, *i.e.*, before he has made the very least judgment about it or submitted it to the very smallest determination by thinking. What thus passes initially through our minds and what our minds pass through—*this* incoherent picture which is not yet differentiated into particular elements, in which nothing seems distinguished from, nothing related to, nothing determined by, anything else, this is the Immediately-Given. On this level of existence—if the phrase is permissible—no object, no event, is as yet more important or more significant than any other. The rudimentary organ of an animal, which, in the light of the knowledge belonging to a higher level of existence, is perhaps seen to be without any importance whatever for the development and life of the animal, comes before us with the same claim to our attention as the noblest and most necessary part of the organism. *Prior* to all cognitive activity nothing in our picture of the world appears as substance, nothing as quality, nothing as cause or as effect. The contrasts of matter and spirit, of body and soul, have not yet arisen. Every other predicate, too, must be kept away from the world-picture presented at this level. We may think of it neither as reality nor as appearance, neither as subjective nor as objective, neither as necessary nor as contingent. We cannot decide at this stage whether it is "thing-in-itself" or mere "idea." For, we have seen already that the conclusions of Physics and Physiology, which lead us to subsume the Given under one or other of the above heads, must not be made the basis on which to build the Theory of Knowledge.

Suppose a being with fully-developed human intelligence were to be suddenly created out of Nothing and confronted with the world, the *first* impression made by the world on his senses and his thought would be pretty much what we have here called the immediately-given world-picture. Of course, no actual man at any moment of his life has nothing but this original world-picture before him. In his mental development there is nowhere a sharp line between pure, passive reception of the Given from without and the cognitive apprehension of it by Thought. This fact might suggest critical doubts concerning our method of determining the starting-point of the Theory of Knowledge. Thus, *e.g.*, Eduard von Hartmann remarks: "We do not ask what is the content of consciousness of a child just awakening to conscious life, nor of an animal on the lowest rung of the ladder of organisms. For, of these things philosophising man has no experience, and, if he tries to reconstruct the content of consciousness of beings on primitive biogenetic or ontogenetic levels, he cannot but base his conclusions on his own personal experience. Hence, our first task is to determine what is the content of consciousness which philosophising man discovers in himself when he begins his philosophical reflection."[1] But, the objection to this view is that the picture of the world with which we begin philosophical reflection, is already qualified by predicates which are the results solely of knowledge. We have no right to accept these predicates without question. On the contrary, we must carefully extract them from out of the world-picture, in order that it may appear in its purity without any admixture due to the process of cognition. In general, the dividing line between what is given and what is added by cognition cannot be identified with any single moment of human development, but must be drawn *artificially*. But this can be done at every level of development, provided only we divide correctly what is presented to us prior to cognition, without any determination by thinking, from what is made of it by cognition.

Now, it may be objected that we have already piled up a whole host of thought-determinations in the very process of extracting the alleged primitive world-picture out of the complete picture into which man's cognitive elaboration has transformed it. But, in defence we must urge that all our conceptual apparatus was employed, not for the characterisation of the primitive world-picture, nor for the determination of its qualities, but solely for the guidance of our analysis, in order to lead it to the point where knowledge recognises that it began. Hence, there can be no question of the truth or error, correctness or incorrectness, of the reflections which, according to our view, precede the moment which brings us to the starting-point of the Theory of Knowledge. Their purpose is solely to guide us *conveniently* to that point. Nobody who is about to occupy himself with epistemological problems, stands at the same time at what we have rightly called the starting-point of knowledge, for his knowledge is already, up to a certain degree, developed. Nothing but analysis with the help of concepts enables us to eliminate from our developed knowledge all the gains of cognitive activity and to determine the starting-point which precedes all such activity. But the concepts thus employed have no cognitive value. They have the purely negative task to eliminate out of our field of vision whatever is the result of cognitive activity and to lead us to the point where this activity first begins. The present discussions point the way to those primitive beginnings upon which the cognitive activity sets to work, but they form no part of such activity. Thus, whatever Theory of Knowledge has to say in the process of determining the starting-point, must be judged, not as true or false, but only as fit or unfit for this purpose. Error is excluded, too, from that starting-point itself. For, error can begin only with the activity of cognition; prior to this, it cannot occur.

This last proposition is compatible only with the kind of Theory of Knowledge which sets out from our line of thought. For, a theory which sets out from some object (or subject) with a definite conceptual determination is liable to error from the very start, viz., in this very determination. Whether this determination is justified or not, depends on the laws which the cognitive act establishes. This is a question to which only the course of the epistemological inquiry itself can supply the answer. All error is excluded only when I can say that I have eliminated all conceptual determinations which are the results of my cognitive activity, and that I retain nothing but what enters the circle of my experience without any activity on my part. Where, on principle, I abstain from every positive affirmation, there I cannot fall into error.

From the epistemological point of view, *error can occur only within the sphere of cognitive activity*. An illusion of the senses is no error. The fact that the rising moon appears to us bigger than the moon overhead is not an error, but a phenomenon fully explained by the laws of nature. An error would result only, if thought, in ordering the data of perception, were to put a false interpretation on the "bigger" or "smaller" size of the moon. But such an interpretation would lie *within* the sphere of cognitive activity.

If knowledge is really to be understood in its essential nature, we must, without doubt, begin our study of it at the point where it originates, where it starts. Moreover, it is clear that whatever *precedes* its starting-point has no legitimate place in any explanatory Theory of Knowledge, but must simply be taken for granted. It is the task of science, in its several branches, to study the essential nature of all that we are here taking for granted. Our aim, here, is not to acquire specific knowledge of this or that, but to investigate knowledge as such. We must first understand the act of cognition, before we can judge what significance to attach to the affirmations about the content of the world which come to be made in the process of getting to know that content.

For this reason, we abstain from every attempt to determine what is immediately-given, so long as we are ignorant of the relation of our determinations to what is determined by them. Not even the concept of the "immediately-given" affirms any positive determination of what precedes cognition. Its only purpose is to point towards the Given, to direct our attention upon it. Here, at the starting-point of the Theory of Knowledge, the term merely expresses, in conceptual form, the initial relation of the cognitive activity to the world-content. The choice of this term allows even for the case that the whole world-content should turn out to be nothing but a figment of our own "Ego," *i.e.*, that the most extreme subjectivism should be right. For, of course, subjectivism does not express a fact which is *given*. It can, at best, be only the result of theoretical considerations. Its truth, in other words, needs to be established by the Theory of Knowledge. It cannot serve as the presupposition of that theory.

This immediately-given world-content includes everything which can appear within the horizon of our experience, in the widest sense of this term, viz., sensations, percepts, intuitions, feelings, volitions, dreams, fancies, representations, concepts, ideas.

Illusions, too, and hallucinations stand at this level exactly on a par with other elements of the world-content. Only theoretical considerations can teach us in what relations illusions, etc., stand to other percepts.

A Theory of Knowledge which starts from the assumption that all the experiences just enumerated are contents of our consciousness, finds itself confronted at once by the question: How do we transcend our consciousness so as to apprehend reality? Where is the jumping-board which will launch us from the subjective into the trans-subjective? For us, the situation is quite different. For us, consciousness and the idea of the "Ego" are, primarily, only items in the Immediately-Given, and the relation of the latter to the two former has first to be discovered by knowledge. We do not start from consciousness in order to determine the nature of knowledge, but, *vice versa*, we start from knowledge in order to determine consciousness and the relation of subject to object. Seeing that, at the outset, we attach no predicates whatever to the Given, we are bound to ask: How is it that we are able to determine it at all? How is it possible to start knowledge anywhere at all? How do we come to designate one item of the world-content, as, *e.g.*, percept, another as concept, a third as reality, others as appearance, as cause, as effect? How do we come to differentiate ourselves from what is "objective," and to contrast "Ego" and "Non-Ego?"

We must discover the bridge which leads from the picture of the world as given to the picture of it which our cognitive activity unfolds. But the following difficulty confronts us. So long as we do nothing but passively gaze at the Given, we can nowhere find a point which knowledge can take hold of and from which it can develop its interpretations. Somewhere in the Given we must discover the spot where we can get to work, where something homogeneous to cognition meets us. If everything were *merely* given, we should never get beyond the bare gazing outwards into the external world and a no less bare gazing inwards into the privacy of our inner world. We should, at most, be able to *describe*, but never to *understand*, the objects outside of us. Our concepts would stand in a purely external, not in an internal, relation to that to which they apply. If there is to be knowledge, everything depends on there being, somewhere within the Given, a field in which our cognitive activity does not merely presuppose the Given, but is at work in the very heart of the Given itself. In other words, the very strictness with which we hold fast the Given, as merely given, must reveal that not everything is given. Our demand for the Given turns out to have been one which, in being strictly maintained, partially cancels itself. We have insisted on the demand, lest we should arbitrarily fix upon some point as the starting-point of the Theory of Knowledge, instead of making a genuine effort to discover it. In our sense of the word "given," everything may be given, *even what in its own innermost nature is not given*. That is to say, the latter presents itself, in that case, to us purely *formally* as given, but reveals itself, on closer inspection, for what it really is.

The whole difficulty in understanding knowledge lies in that we do not create the world-content out of ourselves. If we did so create it, there would be no knowledge at all. Only objects which are given can occasion questions for me. Objects which I create receive their determinations *by my act*. Hence, I do not need to ask whether these determinations are true or false.

This, then, is the second point in our Theory of Knowledge. It consists in the postulate that there must, within the sphere of the Given, be a point at which our activity does not float in a vacuum, at which the world-content itself enters into our activity.

We have already determined the starting-point of the Theory of Knowledge by assigning it a place wholly *antecedent* to all cognitive activity, lest we should distort that activity by some prejudice borrowed from among its own results. Now we determine the first step in the development of our knowledge in such a way that, once more, there can be no question of error or incorrectness. For, we affirm no judgment about anything whatsoever, but merely state the condition which must be fulfilled if knowledge is to be acquired at all. It is all-important that we should, with the most complete critical self-consciousness, keep before our minds the fact that we are postulating the very character which that part of the world-content must possess on which our cognitive activity can begin to operate.

Nothing else is, in fact, possible. As given, the world-content is wholly without determinations. No part of it can by itself furnish the impulse for order to begin to be introduced into the chaos. Hence, cognitive activity must issue its edict and declare what the character of that part is to be. Such an edict in no way infringes the character of the Given as such. It introduces no arbitrary affirmation into science. For, in truth, it affirms nothing. It merely declares that, if the possibility of knowledge is to be explicable at all, we need to look for a field like the one above described. If there is such a field, knowledge can be explained; if not, not. We began our Theory of Knowledge with the "Given" as a whole; now we limit our requirement to the singling out of a particular field within the Given.

Let us come to closer grips with this requirement. Where within the world-picture do we find something which is not merely given, but is given only in so far as it is at the same time created by the cognitive activity?

We need to be absolutely clear that this creative activity must, in its turn, be given to us in all its immediacy. No inferences must be required in order to know that it occurs. Thence it follows, at once, that sense-data do not meet our requirement. For, the fact that they do not occur without our activity is known to us, not immediately, but as an inference from physical and physiological arguments. On the other hand, we do know immediately that it is only in and through the cognitive act that concepts and ideas enter into the sphere of the Immediately-Given. Hence, no one is deceived concerning the character of concepts and ideas. It is possible to mistake a hallucination for an object given from without, but no one is ever likely to believe that his concepts are given without the activity of his own thinking. A lunatic will regard as real, though they are in fact unreal, only things and relations which have attached to them the predicate of "actuality," but he will never say of his concepts and ideas that they have come into the world without his activity. Everything else in our world-picture is such that it must be *given*, if it is to be experienced by us. Only of our concepts and ideas is the opposite true: *they must be produced by us, if they are to be experienced.* They, and only they, are given in a way which might be called *intellectual intuition*. Kant and the modern philosophers who follow him deny altogether that man possesses this kind of intuition, on the ground that all our thinking refers solely to objects and is absolutely impotent to produce anything out of itself, whereas in intellectual intuition form and matter must be given together. But, is not precisely this actually the case with pure concepts and ideas?[2] To see this, we must consider them purely in the form in which, as yet, they are quite free from all empirical content. In order, *e.g.*, to comprehend the pure concept of causality, we must go, not to a particular instance of causality nor to the sum of all instances, but to the pure concept itself. Particular causes and effects must be discovered by investigation in the world, but *causality as a Form* of Thought must be created by ourselves before we can discover causes in the world. If we hold fast to Kant's thesis that concepts without percepts are empty, it becomes unintelligible how the determination of the Given by concepts is to be possible. For, suppose there are given two items of the world-content, *a* and *b*. In order to find a relation between them, I must be guided in my search by a rule of determinate content. Such a rule I can only create in the act of cognition itself. I cannot derive it from the object, because it is only with the help of the rule that the object is to receive its determinations. Such a rule, therefore, for the determination of the real has its being wholly in purely conceptual form.

Before passing on, we must meet a possible objection. It might seem as if in our argument we had unconsciously assigned a prominent part to the idea of the "Ego," or the "personal subject," and as if we employed this idea in the development of our line of thought, without having established our right to do so. For example, we have said that "*we* produce concepts," or that "*we* make this or that demand." But these are mere forms of speech which play no part in our argument. That the cognitive act is the act of, and originates in, an "Ego," can, as we have already pointed out, be affirmed only as an inference in the process of knowledge itself. Strictly, we ought at the outset to speak only of cognitive activity without so much as mentioning a cognitive agent. For, all that has been established so far amounts to no more than this, (1) that something is "given," and (2) that at a certain point within the "given" there originates the postulate set forth above; also, that concepts and ideas are the entities which answer to that postulate. This is not to deny that the point at which the postulate originates is the "Ego." But, in the first instance, we are content to establish these two steps in the Theory of Knowledge in their abstract purity.

1

Das Grundproblem der Erkenntnistheorie, p. 1.

2

By "concept" I mean a rule for the synthesis of the disconnected data of perception into a unity. Causality, *e.g.*, is a "concept." By "idea" I mean nothing but a concept of richer connotation. "Organism," taken quite generally, is an example of an "idea."

V

KNOWLEDGE AND REALITY

Concepts and ideas, then, though themselves part of the Given, yet at the same time take us beyond the Given. Thus, they make it possible to determine also the nature of the other modes of cognitive activity.

By means of a postulate, we have selected a special part out of the given world-picture, because it is the very essence of knowledge to proceed from a part with just this character. Thus, we have made the selection solely in order to be able to understand knowledge. But, we must clearly confess to ourselves that by this selection we have artificially torn in two the unity of the given world-picture. We must bear in mind that the part which we have divorced from the Given still continues, quite apart from our postulate and independently of it, to stand in a necessary connection with the world as given. This fact determines the next step forward in the Theory of Knowledge. It will consist in restoring the unity which we have destroyed in order to show how knowledge is possible. This restoration will consist in *thinking* about the world as given. The act of thinking about the world actually effects the synthesis of the two parts of the given world-content—of the Given which we survey up to the horizon of our experience, and of the part which, in order to be also given, must be produced by us in the activity of cognition. The cognitive act is the synthesis of these two factors. In every single cognitive act the one factor appears as something produced in the act itself and as added to the other factor which is the pure datum. It is only at the very start of the Theory of Knowledge that the factor which otherwise appears as always produced, appears also as given.

To *think* about the world is to transmute the given world by means of concepts and ideas. Thinking, thus, is in very truth the act which brings about knowledge. Knowledge can arise only if thinking, out of itself, introduces order into the content of the world as given. Thinking is itself an activity which produces a content of its own in the moment of cognition. Hence, the content cognised, in so far as it has its origin solely in thinking, offers no difficulty to cognition. We need only observe it, for in its essential nature it is immediately given to us. The *description* of thinking is also the science of thinking. In fact, Logic was never anything but a description of the forms of thinking, never a demonstrative science. For, demonstration occurs only when there is a synthesis of the products of thinking with a content otherwise given. Hence, Gideon Spicker is quite right when he says in his book, *Lessing's Weltanschauung* (p. 5): "We have no means of knowing, either empirically or logically, whether the results of thinking, as such, are true." We may add that, since demonstration already presupposes thinking, thinking itself cannot be demonstrated. We can demonstrate a particular fact, but we cannot demonstrate the process of demonstrating itself. We can only describe what a demonstration is. All logical theory is wholly empirical. Logic is a science which consists only of observation. But if we want to get to know anything over and above our thinking, we can do so only with the help of thinking. That is to say, our thinking must apply itself to something given and transform its chaotic into a systematic connection with the world-picture. Thinking, then, in its application to the world as given, is a formative principle. The process is as follows. First, thinking selects certain details out of the totality of the Given. For, in the Given, there are strictly no individual details, but only an undifferentiated continuum. Next, thinking relates the selected details to each other according to the forms which it has itself produced. And, lastly, it determines what follows from this relation. The act of relating two distinct items of the world-content to each other does not imply that thinking arbitrarily determines something about them. Thinking waits and sees what is the spontaneous consequence of the relation established. With this consequence we have at last some degree of knowledge of the two selected items of the world-content. Suppose the world-content reveals nothing of its nature in response to the establishment of such a relation, then the effort of thinking must miscarry, and a fresh effort must take its place. All cognitions consist in this, that two or more items of the Given are brought into relation with each other by us and that we apprehend what follows from this relation.

Without doubt, many of our efforts of thinking miscarry, not only in the sciences, as is amply proved by their history, but also in ordinary life. But in the simple cases of mistake which are, after all, the commonest, the correct thought so rapidly replaces the incorrect, that the latter is never, or rarely, noticed.

Kant, in his theory of the "synthetic unity of apperception," had an inkling of this activity of thought in the systematic organisation of the world-content, as we have here developed it. But his failure to appreciate clearly the real function of thinking is revealed by the fact, that he believes himself able to deduce the *a priori* laws of Pure Natural Science from the rules according to which this synthetic activity proceeds. Kant has overlooked that the synthetic activity of thinking is merely the preparation for the discovery of natural laws properly so-called. Suppose we select two items, *a* and *b*, from the Given. For knowledge to arise of a nexus according to law between *a* and *b*, the first requirement is that thinking should so relate *a* and *b*, that the relation may appear to us as given. Thus, the content proper of the law of nature is derived from what is given, and the sole function of thinking is to establish such relations between the items of the world-picture that the laws to which they are subject become manifest. The pure synthetic activity of thinking is not the source of any objective laws whatever.

We must inquire what part thinking plays in the formation of our scientific world-picture as distinct from the merely given one. It follows from our account that thinking supplies the formal principle of the conformity of phenomena to law. Suppose, in our example above, that *a* is the cause, *b* the effect. Unless thinking were able to produce the concept of causality, we should never be able to know that *a* and *b* were causally connected. But, in order that we may know, in the given case, that *a* is the cause and *b* the effect, it is necessary for *a* and *b* to possess the characteristics which we mean when we speak of cause and effect. A similar analysis applies to the other categories of thought.

It will be appropriate to notice here in a few words Hume's discussion of causality. According to Hume, the concepts of cause and effect have their origin solely in *custom*. We observe repeatedly that one event follows another and become accustomed to think of them as causally connected, so that we expect the second to occur as soon as we have observed the first.

This theory, however, springs from a totally mistaken view of the causal relation. Suppose for several days running I observe the same person whenever I step out of the door of my house, I shall gradually form the habit of expecting the temporal sequence of the two events. But, it will never occur to me to think that there is any causal connection between my own appearance and that of the other person at the same spot. I shall call in aid essentially other items of the world-content in order to explain the coincidence of these events. In short, we determine the causal nexus of two events, not according to their temporal sequence, but according to the essential character of the items of the world-content which we call, respectively, cause and effect.

From this purely formal activity of our thinking in the construction of the scientific picture of the world, it follows that the content of every cognition cannot be fixed *a priori* in advance of observation (in which thinking comes to grips with the Given), but must be derived completely and exhaustively from observation. In this sense, all our cognitions are empirical. Nor is it possible to see how it could be otherwise. For, Kant's judgments *a priori* are at bottom, not cognitions, but postulates. On Kant's principles, all we can ever say is only this, that if a thing is to become the object of possible experience, it must conform to these laws. They are, therefore, rules which the subject prescribes to all objects. But, we should rather expect cognitions of the Given to have their source, not in the constitution of the subject, but in that of the object.

Thinking makes no *a priori* affirmations about the Given. But it creates the forms, on the basis of which the conformity of phenomena to law becomes manifest *a posteriori*.

From our point of view, it is impossible to determine anything *a priori* about the degree of certainty belonging to a judgment which embodies knowledge thus gained. For, certainty, too, derives from nothing other than the Given. Perhaps it will be objected that observation never establishes anything except that a certain nexus of phenomena actually occurs, but not that it must occur, and will always occur, in like conditions. But, this suggestion, too, is in error. For any nexus which I apprehend between elements in the world-picture is, on our principles, nothing but what is grounded in these elements themselves. It is not imported into these elements by thinking, but belongs to them essentially, and must, therefore, necessarily exist whenever they themselves exist.

Only a view which regards all scientific research as nothing but the endeavour to correlate the facts of experience by means of principles which are subjective and external to the facts, can hold that the nexus of a and b may to-day obey one law and to-morrow another (J. S. Mill). On the other hand, if we see clearly that the laws of nature have their source in the Given, and that, therefore, the nexus of phenomena essentially depends upon, and is determined by, them, we shall never think of talking of a "merely relative universality" of the laws which are derived from observation. This is, of course, not to assert that any given law which we have once accepted as correct, must be absolutely valid. But when, later, a negative instance overthrows a law, the reason is, not that the law from the first could be inferred only with relative universality, but that it had not at first been inferred correctly. A genuine law of nature is nothing but the formulation of a nexus in the given world-picture, and it exists as little without the facts which it determines, as these exist without it.

Above, we have laid down that it is the essence of the cognitive activity to transmute, by thinking, the given world-picture by means of concepts and ideas. What follows from this fact? If the Immediately-Given were a totality complete in itself, the work which thinking does upon it in cognition would be both impossible and unnecessary. We should simply accept the Given, as it is, and be satisfied with it as such. Cognitive activity is possible only because in the Given something lies hidden which does *not* yet reveal itself so long as we gaze at the Given in its immediacy, but which becomes manifest with the aid of the order which thinking introduces. Prior to the work of thinking, the Given does not possess the fulness of its own complete nature.

This point becomes still more obvious by considering in greater detail the two factors involved in the act of cognition. The first factor is the Given. "Being given" is not a quality of the Given, but merely a term expressing its relation to the second factor in the act of cognition. This second factor, viz., the conceptual content of the Given, is found by our thought in the act of cognition to be necessarily connected with the Given. Two questions arise: (1) Where are the Given and the Concept differentiated? (2) Where are they united? The answer to these two questions is to be found, beyond any doubt, in the preceding discussions. They are differentiated solely in the act of cognition. They are united in the Given. Thence it follows necessarily that the conceptual content is but a part of the Given, and that the act of cognition consists in re-uniting with each other the two parts of the world-picture which are, at first, given to it in separation. The given world-picture thus attains its completion only through that mediate kind of givenness which thinking brings about. In its original immediacy the world-picture is altogether incomplete.

If the conceptual content were from the first united with the Given in our world-picture, there would be no cognition. For, no need could ever arise of transcending the Given. So, again, if by thinking and in thinking we could create the whole world-content, once more there would be no cognition. For, what we create ourselves we do not need to cognise. Hence, cognition exists because the world-content is given to us originally in a form which is incomplete, which does not contain it as a whole, but which, over and above what it presents immediately, owns another, no less essential, aspect. This second aspect of the world-content—an aspect not originally given—is revealed by cognition. Pure thinking presents in the abstract, not empty forms, but a sum of determinations (categories) which serve as forms for the rest of the world-content. *The world-content can be called REALITY only in the form which it acquires through cognition and in which both aspects of it are united.*

VI

THEORY OF KNOWLEDGE WITHOUT PRESUPPOSITIONS *VERSUS* FICHTE'S THEORY OF SCIENCE

So far, we have determined the idea of knowledge. This idea is given immediately in the human consciousness whenever it functions cognitively. To the "Ego," as the centre[1] of consciousness, are given immediately external and internal perceptions, as well as its own existence. The Ego feels impelled to find more in the Given than it *immediately* contains. Over against the given world, a second world, the world of thinking, unfolds itself for the Ego and the Ego unites these two by realising, of its own free will, the idea of knowledge which we have determined. This accounts for the fundamental difference between the way in which in the objects of human consciousness itself the concept and the Immediately-Given unite to form Reality in its wholeness, and the way in which their union obtains in the rest of the world-content. For every other part of the world-content we must assume that the union of the two factors is original and necessary from the first, and that it is *only for cognition,* when cognition begins, that an artificial separation has supervened, but that cognition in the end undoes the separation in keeping with the original and essential unity of the object-world. For consciousness the case is quite otherwise. Here the union exists only when it is achieved by the living activity of consciousness itself. With every other kind of object, the separation of the two factors is significant, not for the object, but only for knowledge. Their union is here original, their separation derivative. Cognition effects a separation only because it must first separate before it can achieve union by its own methods. But, for consciousness, the Concept and the Given are originally separate. Union is here derivative, and that is why cognition has the character which we have described. Just because in consciousness Idea and Given appear in separation, does the whole of reality split itself for consciousness into these two factors. And, again, just because consciousness can bring about the union of the two factors only by its own activity, can it reach full reality only by performing the act of cognition. The remaining categories (ideas) would be necessarily united with the corresponding lands of the Given, even if they were not taken up into cognition. But the idea of cognition can be united with the Given which corresponds to it, only by the activity of consciousness. *Real* consciousness exists only in realising itself. With these remarks we believe ourselves to be sufficiently equipped for laying bare the root-error of Fichte's *Wissenschaftslehre* and, at the same time, for supplying the key to the understanding of it. Fichte is among all Kant's successors the one who has felt most vividly that nothing but a theory of consciousness can supply the foundation for all the sciences. But he never clearly understood why this is so. He felt that the act which we have called the second step in the Theory of Knowledge and which we have formulated as a postulate, must really be performed by the "Ego." This may be seen, *e.g.*, from the following passage. "The Theory of Science, then, arises, as itself a systematic discipline, just as do all possible sciences in so far as they are systematic, through a certain act of freedom, the determinate function of which is, more particularly, to make us conscious of the characteristic activity of intelligence as such. The result of this free act is that the necessary activity of intelligence, which in itself already is form, is further taken up as matter into a fresh form of cognition or consciousness."[2] What does Fichte here mean by the activity of the "intelligence," when we translate what he has obscurely felt into clear concepts? Nothing but the realisation of the idea of knowledge, taking place in consciousness. Had this been perfectly clear to Fichte, he ought to have expressed his view simply by saying, "It is the task of the Theory of Science to bring cognition, in so far as it is still an unreflective activity of the 'Ego,' into reflective consciousness; it has to show that the realisation of the idea of cognition in actual fact is a necessary activity of the 'Ego.'"

Fichte tries to determine the activity of the "Ego." He declares "that the being, the essence of which consists solely in this that it posits itself as existing, is the Ego as absolute subject."[3] This positing of the Ego is for Fichte the original, unconditioned act "which lies at the basis of all the rest of consciousness."[4] It follows that the Ego, in Fichte's sense, can likewise begin all its activity only through an absolute fiat of the will. But, it is impossible for Fichte to supply any sort of content for this activity which his "Ego" absolutely posits. For, Fichte can name nothing upon which this activity might direct itself, or by which it might be determined. His Ego is supposed to perform an act. Yes, but *what* is it to do? Fichte failed to define the concept of cognition which the Ego is to realise, and, in consequence, he struggled in vain to find any way of advancing from his absolute act to the detailed determinations of the Ego. Nay, in the end he declares that the inquiry into the manner of this advance lies outside the scope of his theory. In his deduction of the idea of cognition he starts neither from an absolute act of the Ego, nor from one of the Non-Ego, but from a state of being determined which is, at the same time, an act of determining. His reason for this is that nothing else either is, or can be, immediately contained in consciousness. His theory leaves it wholly vague what determines, in turn, this determination. And it is this vagueness which drives us on beyond Fichte's theory into the practical part of the *Wissenschaftslehre*.[5] But, by this turn Fichte destroys all knowledge whatsoever. For, the practical activity of the Ego belongs to quite a different sphere. The postulate which we have put forward above can, indeed, be realised—so much is clear—only by a free act of the Ego. But, if this act is to be a cognitive act, the all-important point is that its voluntary decision should be to realise the idea of cognition. It is, no doubt, true that the Ego by its own free will can do many other things as well. But, what matters for the epistemological foundation of the sciences is not a definition of what it is for the Ego to be *free*, but of what it is to *know*. Fichte has allowed himself to be too much influenced by his subjective tendency to present the freedom of human personality in the brightest light. Harms, in his address on *The Philosophy of Fichte* (p. 15), rightly remarks, "His world-view is predominantly and exclusively ethical, and the same character is exhibited by his Theory of Knowledge." Knowledge would have absolutely nothing to do, if all spheres of reality were given in their totality. But, seeing that the Ego, so long as it has not been, by thinking, inserted into its place in the systematic whole of the world-picture, exists merely as an immediately-given something, it is not enough merely to point out what it does. Fichte, however, believes that all we need to do concerning the Ego is to *seek and find* it. "We have to *seek and find* the absolutely first, wholly unconditioned principle of all human knowledge. Being absolutely first, this principle admits neither of *proof* nor of *determination*."[6] We have seen that proof and determination are out of place solely as applied to the content of Pure Logic. But the Ego is a part of reality, and this makes it necessary to establish that this or that category is actually to be found in the Given. Fichte has failed to do this. And this is the reason why he has given such a mistaken form to his Theory of Science. Zeller remarks[7] that the logical formulæ by means of which Fichte seeks to reach the concept of the Ego, do but ill disguise his predetermined purpose at any price to reach this starting-point for his theory. This comment applies to the first form (1794) which Fichte gave to his *Wissenschaftslehre*. Taking it, then, as established that Fichte, in keeping with the whole trend of his philosophical thinking, could not, in fact, rest content with any other starting-point for knowledge than an absolute and arbitrary act, we have the choice between only two ways of making this start intelligible. The one way was to seize upon some one among the empirical activities of consciousness and to strip off, one by one, all the characteristics of it which do not follow originally from its essential nature, until the pure concept of the Ego had been crystallised out. The other way was to begin, straightway, with the original activity of the Ego, and to exhibit its nature by introspection and reflection. Fichte followed the first way at the outset of his philosophical thinking, but in the course of it he gradually switched over to the other.

Basing himself upon Kant's "synthesis of transcendental apperception," Fichte concluded that the whole activity of the Ego in the synthesis of the matter of experience proceeds according to the forms of the judgment. To judge is to connect a predicate with a subject—an act of which the purely formal expression is $a = a$. This proposition would be impossible if the x which connects predicate and subject, did not rest upon a power to affirm unconditionally. For, the proposition does not mean, "a exists"; it means, "if a exists, then there exists a." Thus, a is most certainly not affirmed absolutely. Hence, if there is to be an absolute, unconditionally valid affirmation, there is no alternative but to declare the act of affirming itself to be absolute. Whereas a is conditioned, the affirming of a is unconditioned. This affirming is the act of the Ego which, thus, possesses the power to affirm absolutely and without conditions. In the proposition, a

= *a*, the one *a* is affirmed only on condition of the other being presupposed. Moreover, the affirming is an act of the Ego. "If *a* is affirmed in the Ego, it is affirmed."[8] This connection is possible only on condition that there is in the Ego something always self-identical, which effects the transition from the one *a* to the other. The above-mentioned *x* is this self-identical aspect of the Ego. The Ego which affirms the one *a* is the same Ego as that which affirms the other *a*. This is to say Ego = Ego. But this proposition, expressed in judgment-form, "If the Ego is, it is," is meaningless. For, the Ego is not affirmed on condition of another Ego having been presupposed, but it presupposes itself. In short, the Ego is absolute and unconditioned. The hypothetical judgment-form which is the form of all judgments, so long as the absolute Ego is not presupposed, changes for the Ego into the form of the categorical affirmation of existence, "*I am* unconditionally." Fichte has another way of putting this: "the Ego originally affirms its own existence."[9] Clearly, this whole deduction is nothing but a sort of elementary school-drill by means of which Fichte tries to lead his readers to the point at which they will perceive for themselves the unconditioned activity of the Ego. His aim is to put clearly before their eyes that fundamental activity of the Ego in the absence of which there is no such thing as an Ego at all.

Let us now look back, once more, over Fichte's line of thought. On closer inspection, it becomes obvious that it contains a leap—a leap, moreover, which throws grave doubts upon the correctness of his theory of the original act of the Ego. What precisely is it that is absolute in the affirmation of the Ego? Take the judgment, "If *a* exists, then there exists *a*." The *a* is affirmed by the Ego. So far there is no room for doubt. But, though the act is unconditioned, yet the Ego must affirm *something in particular*. It cannot affirm an "activity in general and as such"; it can affirm only a particular, determinate activity. In short, the affirmation must have a content. But, it cannot derive this content from itself, for else we should get nothing but affirmations of acts of affirmation *in infinitum*. Hence, there must be something which is realised by this affirming, by this absolute activity of the Ego. If the Ego does not seize upon something given in order to affirm it, it can do *nothing* at all, and, consequently, it *cannot* affirm either. This is proved, too, by Fichte's proposition, "the Ego affirms its own existence." "Existence," here, is a category. Thus, we are back at our own position: the activity of the Ego consists in that it affirms, of its own free will, the concepts and ideas inherent in the Given. If Fichte had not unconsciously been determined to exhibit the Ego as "existing," he would have got nowhere at all. If, instead, he had built up the concept of cognition, he would have reached the true starting-point of the Theory of Knowledge, viz., "The Ego affirms the act of cognition." Because Fichte failed to make clear to himself what determines the activity of the Ego, he fixed simply upon the affirmation of its own existence as the character of that activity. But, this is at once to restrict the absolute activity of the Ego. For, if nothing is unconditioned except the Ego's affirmation of its own existence, then every other activity of the Ego is conditioned. Moreover, the way is cut off for passing from the unconditioned to the conditioned. If the Ego is unconditioned only in the affirmation of its own existence, then at once there is cut off all possibility of affirming by an original act anything other than its own existence. Hence, the necessity arises to assign a ground for all the other activities of the Ego. But Fichte, as we have seen above, sought for such a ground in vain.

This is the reason why he shifted to the second of the two ways, indicated above, for the deduction of the Ego. Already in 1797, in his *Erste Einleitung in die Wissenschaftslehre*, he recommends self-observation as the right method for studying the Ego in its true, original character. "Observe and watch thyself, turn thy eye away from all that surrounds thee and look into thyself—this is the first demand which philosophy makes upon its disciple. The topic of our discourse, is, not anything outside thyself, but thyself alone."[10] This introduction to the Theory of Science is, in truth, in one way much superior to the other. For, self-observation does not make us acquainted with the activity of the Ego one-sidedly in a fixed direction. It exhibits that activity, not merely as affirming its own existence, but as striving, in its many-sided development, to comprehend by thinking the world-content which is immediately-given. To self-observation, the Ego reveals itself as engaged in building up its world-picture by the synthesis of the Given with concepts. But, anyone who has not accompanied us in our line of thought above, and who, consequently, does not know that the Ego can grasp the whole content of reality only on condition of applying its Thought-Forms to the *Given*, is liable to regard cognition as a mere process of spinning the world out of the Ego itself. Hence, for Fichte the world-picture tends increasingly to become a construction of the Ego. He emphasises more and more that the main point in the *Wissenschaftslehre* is to awaken the sense which is able to watch the Ego in this constructing of its world. He who is able thus to watch stands, for Fichte, on a higher level of knowledge than he who has eyes only for the finished construct, the ready-made world. If we fix our eyes only on the world of objects, we fail to perceive that, but for the creative activity of the Ego, that world would not exist. If, on the other hand, we watch the Ego in its constructive activity, we understand the *ground* of the finished world-picture. We know how it has come to be what it is. We understand it as the conclusion for which we have the premises. The ordinary consciousness sees only what has been affirmed, what has been determined thus or thus. It lacks the insight into the premises, into the grounds why an affirmation is just as it is and not otherwise. To mediate the knowledge of these premises is, according to Fichte, the task of a wholly new sense. This is expressed most clearly in the *Einleitungsvorlesungen in die Wissenschaftslehre*.[11] "My theory presupposes a wholly novel inward sense-organ, by means of which a new world is given which does not exist for the ordinary man at all." Or, again, "The world of this novel sense, and thereby this sense itself, are hereby for the present clearly determined: it is the world in which we see the premises on which is grounded the judgment, 'Something exists'; it is the *ground* of existence which, just because it is the ground of existence, cannot, in its turn, be said to be or to be an existence."[12]

But, here, too, Fichte lacks clear insight into the activity of the Ego. He has never worked his way through to it. That is why his *Wissenschaftslehre* could not become what else, from its whole design, it ought to have become, viz., a Theory of Knowledge as the fundamental discipline of philosophy. For, after it had once been recognised that the activity of the Ego must be *affirmed* by the Ego itself, it was very easy to think that the activity receives its determination also from the Ego. But how else can this happen except we assign a content to the purely formal activity of the Ego? If the Ego is really to import a content into its activity which, else, is wholly undetermined, then the nature of that content must also be determined. For, failing this, it could at best be realised only by some "thing-in-itself" in the

Ego, of which the Ego would be the instrument, but not by the Ego itself. If Fichte had attempted to furnish this determination, he would have been led to the concept of cognition which it is the task of the Ego to realise. Fichte's *Wissenschaftslehre* proves that even the acutest thinker fails to make fruitful contributions to any philosophical discussion, unless he lays hold of the correct Thought-Form (category, idea) which, supplemented by the Given, yields reality. Such a thinker is like a man who fails to hear the most glorious melodies which are being played for him, because he has no ear for tunes. If we are to determine the nature of consciousness, as given, we must be able to rise to, and make our own, the "idea of consciousness."

At one point Fichte is actually quite close to the true view. He declares, in the *Einleitungen zur Wissenschaftslehre* (1797), that there are two theoretical systems, viz., Dogmatism, for which the Ego is determined by the objects, and Idealism, for which the objects are determined by the Ego. Both are, according to him, established as possible theories of the world; both can be developed into self-consistent systems. But, if we throw in our lot with Dogmatism, we must abandon the independence of the Ego and make it dependent on the "thing-in-itself." If we do not want to do this, we must adopt Idealism. The philosopher's choice between these two systems is left by Fichte wholly to the preference of the Ego. But he adds that if the Ego desires to preserve its independence, it will give up the belief in external things and surrender itself to Idealism.

But, what Fichte forgot was the consideration that the Ego cannot make any genuine, well-grounded decision or choice, unless something is presupposed which helps the Ego to choose. All the Ego's attempts at determination remain empty and without content, if the Ego does not find something wholly determinate and full of content, which enables it to determine the Given, and thereby also to choose between Idealism and Dogmatism. This "something wholly determinate and full of content" is, precisely, the world of Thought. And the determination of the Given by thinking is, precisely, what we call *cognition*. We may take Fichte where we please—everywhere we find that his line of thought at once gets meaning and substance, as soon as we conceive his grey, empty activity of the Ego to be filled and regulated by what we have called "the process of cognition."

The fact that the Ego is free to enter into activity out of itself, makes it possible for it, by free self-determination, to realise the category of cognition, whereas in the rest of the world all categories are connected by objective necessity with the Given which corresponds to them. The investigation of the nature of free self-determination will be the task of Ethics and Metaphysics, based on our Theory of Knowledge. These disciplines, too, will have to debate the question whether the Ego is able to realise other ideas, besides the idea of cognition. But, that the realisation of the idea of cognition issues from a free act has been made sufficiently clear in the course of our discussions above. For, the synthesis, effected by the Ego, of the Immediately-Given and of the Form of Thought appropriate to it, which two factors of reality remain otherwise always divorced from each other in consciousness, can be brought about only by an act of freedom. Moreover, our arguments throw, in another way, quite a fresh light on Critical Idealism. To any close student of Fichte's system it will appear as if Fichte cared for nothing so much as for the defence of the proposition, that nothing can enter the Ego from without, that nothing can appear in the Ego which was not the Ego's own original creation. Now, it is beyond all dispute that no type of Idealism will ever be able to derive from within the Ego that form of the world-content which we have called "the Immediately-Given." For, this form can only be *given*; it can never be constructed by thinking. In proof of this, it is enough to reflect that, even if the whole series of colours were given to us except one, we should not be able to fill in that *one* out of the bare Ego. We can form an image of the most remote countries, though we have never seen them, provided we have once personally experienced, as given, the details which go to form the image. We then build up the total picture, according to the instructions supplied to us, out of the particular facts which we have ourselves experienced. But we shall strive in vain to invent out of ourselves even a single perceptual element which has never appeared within the sphere of what has been given to us. It is one thing to be merely *acquainted* with the world; it is another to *have knowledge* of its essential nature. This nature, for all that it is closely identified with the world-content, does not become clear to us unless we build up reality ourselves out of the Given and the Forms of Thought. The real "what" of the Given comes to be affirmed for the Ego only through the Ego itself. The Ego would have no occasion to affirm the nature of the Given for itself, if it did not find itself confronted at the outset by the Given in wholly indeterminate form. Thus, the essential nature of the world is affirmed, not *apart* from, but *through,* the Ego.

The true form of reality is not the first form in which it presents itself to the Ego, but the last form which it receives through the activity of the Ego. That first form is, in fact, without any importance for the objective world and counts only as the basis for the process of cognition. Hence, it is not the form given to the world by theory which is *subjective*, but rather the form in which the world is originally given to the Ego. If, following Volkelt and others, we call the given world "experience," our view amounts to saying: The world-picture presents itself, owing to the constitution of our consciousness, in subjective form as experience, but science completes it and makes its true nature manifest.

Our Theory of Knowledge supplies the basis for an Idealism which, in the true sense of the word, understands itself. It supplies good grounds for the conviction that thinking brings home to us the essential nature of the world. Nothing but thinking can exhibit the relations of the parts of the world-content, be it the relation of the heat of the sun to the stone which it warms, or the relation of the Ego to the external world. Thinking alone has the function of determining all things in their relations to each other.

The objection might still be urged by the followers of Kant, that the determination, above-described, of the Given holds, after all, only *for the Ego*. Our reply must be, consistently with our principles, that the distinction between Ego and Outer World, too, holds only within the Given, and that, therefore, it is irrelevant to insist on the phrase, "for the Ego," in the face of the activity of thinking which unites all opposites. The Ego, as divorced from the outer world, disappears completely in the process of thinking out the nature of the world. Hence it becomes meaningless still to talk of determinations which hold *only for the Ego*.

---

[1]

It ought not to be necessary to say that the term "centre," here, is not intended to affirm a theory concerning the nature of consciousness, but is used merely as a shorthand expression for the total physiognomy of consciousness.

2

Fichte's *Sämtliche Werke*, Vol. I, p. 71.

3

l.c., Vol. I, p. 97.

4

l.c., Vol. I, p. 91.

5

l.c., Vol. I, p. 178.

6

l.c., Vol. I, p. 91.

7

Geschichte der Philosophie, p. 605.

8

Fichte, *Sämtliche Werke*, Vol. I, p. 94.

9

l.c., Vol. I, p. 98.

10

l.c., Vol. I, p. 422.

11

Delivered in the autumn of 1813 at the University of Berlin. See *Nachgelassene Werke*, Vol. I, p. 4.

12

l.c., Vol. I, p. 16.

VII

CONCLUDING REMARKS: EPISTEMOLOGICAL

We have laid the foundations of the Theory of Knowledge as the science of the significance of all human knowledge. It alone clears up for us the relation of the contents of the separate sciences to the world. It enables us, with the help of the sciences, to attain to a philosophical world-view. Positive knowledge is acquired by us through particular cognitions; what the value of our knowledge is, considered as knowledge of reality, we learn through the Theory of Knowledge. By holding fast strictly to this principle, and by employing no particular cognitions in our argumentation, we have transcended all one-sided world-views. One-sidedness, as a rule, results from the fact that the inquiry, instead of concentrating on the process of cognition itself, busies itself about some object of that process. If our arguments are sound, *Dogmatism* must abandon its "thing-in-itself" as fundamental principle, and *Subjective Idealism* its "Ego," for both these owe their determinate natures in their relation to each other first to thinking. *Scepticism* must give up its doubts whether the world can be known, for there is no room for doubt with reference to the "Given," because it is as yet untouched by any of the predicates which cognition confers on it. On the other hand, if Scepticism were to assert that thinking can never apprehend things as they are, its assertion, being itself possible only through thinking, would be self-contradictory. For, to justify doubt by thinking is to admit by implication that thinking can produce grounds sufficient to establish certainty. Lastly, our theory of knowledge transcends both one-sided *Empiricism* and one-sided *Rationalism* in uniting both *at a higher level.* Thus it does justice to both. It justifies Empiricism by showing that all *positive* knowledge about the Given is obtainable only through direct contact with the Given. And *Rationalism*, too, receives its due in our argument, seeing that we hold thinking to be the *necessary* and *exclusive* instrument of knowledge.

The world-view which has the closest affinity to ours, as we have here built it up on epistemological foundations, is that of A. E. Biedermann.[1] But

Biedermann requires for the justification of his point of view dogmatic theses which are quite out of place in Theory of Knowledge. Thus, *e.g.*, he works with the concepts of Being, Substance, Space, Time, etc., without having first analysed the cognitive process by itself. Instead of establishing the fact that the cognitive process consists, to begin with, only of the two elements, the Given and Thought, he talks of the *Kinds of Being* of the real. For example, in Section 15, he says: "Every content of consciousness includes within itself two fundamental facts—it presents to us, as given, two kinds of Being which we contrast with each other as sensuous and spiritual, thing-like and idea-like, Being." And in Section 19: "Whatever has a spatio-temporal existence, exists materially; that which is the ground of all existence and the subject of life has an idea-like existence, is real as having an ideal Being." This sort of argument belongs, not to the Theory of Knowledge, but to Metaphysics, which latter presupposes Theory of Knowledge as its foundation. We must admit that Biedermann's doctrine has many points of similarity with ours; but our method has not a single point of contact with his. Hence, we have had no occasion to compare our position directly with his. Biedermann's aim is to gain an epistemological standpoint with the help of a few metaphysical axioms. Our aim is to reach, through an analysis of the process of cognition, a theory of reality.

And we believe that we have succeeded in showing, that all the disputes between philosophical systems result from the fact that their authors have sought to attain knowledge about some object or other (Thing, Self, Consciousness, etc.), without having first given close study to that which alone can throw light on whatever else we know, viz., *the nature of knowledge itself.*

1

cf. his *Christliche Dogmatik*, 2nd edit., 1884–5. The epistemological arguments are in Vol. I. An exhaustive discussion of his point of view has been furnished by E. von Hartmann. See his *Kritische Wanderungen durch die Philosophie der Gegenwart*, pp. 200 ff.

www.ingramcontent.com/pod-product-compliance
Lightning Source LLC
Chambersburg PA
CBHW081107080526
44587CB00021B/3479